Empath Healing

How to Overcome Fear and Develop Your Gift, Becoming a Healer Instead of Absorbing Negative Energies, and Finding Your Sense of Self by Directing Your Potential

RICHARD GOODMIND GOTMAN

Table of Contents

Introduction

Being an empath is when you are affected by other people's energies, and you have an innate ability to intuitively feel and perceive others. Your life is unconsciously influenced by others' desires, wishes, thoughts, moods, and even pain. Being an empath is much more than being highly sensitive and it's not just limited to emotions or physical pain. Empaths can also perceive the motivations and intentions of people around them. Being an empath, you are always open, so to speak, to process other people's feelings and energy. This means that you really feel, and in many cases, take on the emotions of others, sometimes unknowingly.

Many empaths experience things like chronic fatigue, environmental sensitivities, or unexplained aches and pains daily. These are all things that are more likely to be contributed to outside influences and not so much yourself at all. Essentially, you walk around this world with all of the accumulated karma, emotions, and energy from others. Here are the listeners of life. Empathic people are often problem solvers, thinkers, and studiers of many things.

Although many people have heard of empaths, (psychics who are able to sense or feel the emotions of others), few people fully understand what it means to possess empathic psychic abilities.

People naively assume that this ability is a great and wonderful gift, and that it does not come at a cost to the psychic who possesses it. The truth is, this rare talent can also be a deadly burden to bear.

These psychics come wide ranges of sensitivity. On one end of the spectrum are the empathic psychics who can only vaguely recognize other people's feelings, while on the other end there are the powerful psychics who feel people's emotions as though they were their own.

Admittedly, it can be wonderful to be able to understand another person's feelings, and to be able to understand them and to help them cope with their feelings if they need help; empathic psychics are often skilled at emotional healing therapy. This is a process in which the psychic can share the burden of an extreme emotion, thereby lessening the pain that it is causing the patient. Alternatively, a psychic can guide a patient through difficult emotional distress by using their sensitive, intimate understanding of a patient's emotional state of mind.

However, people don't realize that an empathic psychic doesn't necessarily choose weather or not to experience another person's feelings, instead they simply must accept the feelings that come to them. They constantly experiences invasions of their emotional self. They may become confused as to which feelings are their own, and which feelings come from outside sources.

What's worse, an empath usually senses extreme emotions before they experience subtle emotions. As a result, psychics must share the feelings of people in extreme emotional states, rather than the feelings of people in normal emotional states of mind. For an empathic psychic, even something as simple as walking down the street, or going to the grocery store, can be extremely emotionally taxing.

Think about it-having to constantly feel the emotions of others-all the time, and without choosing to can have crippling effects on someone's psyche. Often, empathic psychics "loose themselves" in the feelings of others, and this can lead to self-doubt, confusion, loneliness, and depression.

Psychics who see their ability more as a burden than as a gift should find help by counseling with other empathic psychics who are in similar situations. Having a support network can make living with this ability much more bearable and can significantly improve a psychic's quality of life.

Yes, empaths possess a rare, wonderful gift that has the power to heal and help others, but it comes at an enormous cost.

Chapter 1: Common Traits of an Empath

- ✓ A love of nature & animals
- ✓ Addictive personalities
- ✓ Anal-retentive (hate clutter; no o.c.d.)
- ✓ Can appear moody, shy, aloof, disconnected & unapproachable
- ✓ Creative
- ✓ Daydreamer
- ✓ Defender of the underdog
- ✓ Digestive disorders & lower back problems
- ✓ Drawn to healing, holistic therapies & all things metaphysical
- ✓ Easily bored (need constant stimulation)
- ✓ Electromagnetic sensitivities
- ✓ Empathy (in and of itself)
- ✓ Excellent listeners
- ✓ Fatigue (sometimes chronic; esp. Emotional)
- ✓ Finds routine, rules or control, imprisoning
- ✓ Have a hard time doing things they don't enjoy
- ✓ Intolerance to narcissism & bullies
- ✓ Knowledge-seekers (defenders of the distribution of knowledge)
- ✓ Lovers of adventure, freedom & travel
- ✓ People innately want to confide in them

- ✓ Prefer not to buy/take second-hand items
- ✓ Prone to being overweight, sometimes due to comfort eating
- ✓ Sense the energy of food (many become vegetarian/vegan)
- ✓ Sensitivity to television & movies (particularly violence)
- ✓ Social anxiety (sometimes agoraphobia)
- ✓ Solitary
- ✓ Sympathy pains
- ✓ Truth-seekers (defenders of truth)
- ✓ Walking lie detectors
- ✓ Instinctive (they just know things)

Empaths are loving, caring, kind people who want to help others. They are often found doing volunteer work and may serve others through emotionally-demanding careers as childcare givers, medical professionals, hospice workers, midwives, and such. Most empaths came in with a mission to heal people, animals, plants, and the planet. As healers, many have taken on so much external energy that they spend most of their time trying to clear unwanted energy and recuperate from the last episode that "blew their doors off."

Here are a few characteristics of empaths who have not learned to filter out other people's emotions or manage their own energy:

You constantly feel overwhelmed with emotions and you may cry a lot, feel sad, angry, or depressed for no good reason. You may be tempted to think you are crazy for having random mood swings and bouts of unexplained fatigue. If you are a woman, it's like having PMS all the time! Unrestrained empathy can cause a person to manifest symptoms similar to bipolar (manic-depressive) disorder.

You drop by the store feeling great, but once you get in a crowd you start feeling down, angry, sad, or overwhelmed. You feel you must be coming down with something so you decide to go home and rest.

If you've found that you can't be in public without becoming overwhelmed you may start to live the life of a hermit. But, even at home, you get depressed when you watch the news and you cry while watching a movie. You feel horrible when a commercial for the Humane Society shows animals that need a home. You may rescue more animals than you can possibly care for.

You feel sorry for people no matter who they are or what they have done. You feel the need to stop and help anyone in your path. You can't pass by a homeless person without giving him money-even if you don't have it to spare.

Many empaths are overweight. When they absorb stressful emotions, it can trigger panic attacks, depression as well as food, sex, and drug binges. Some may overeat to cope with emotional stress or use their body weight as a shield or buffer. In Chapter 9 of Yvonne Perry's book, *"Whose Stuff Is This? Finding Freedom from the Thoughts, Feelings, and Energy of Those Around You"*, she shows how to use light as protection.

Most empaths have the ability to physically and emotionally heal others by drawing the pain or ailment out of the sick person and into their own bodies. For obvious reasons, this is not recommended unless you know how to keep from becoming ill in the process.

From chest pains and stomach cramps to migraines and fever, you manifest symptoms without contracting an actual illness. Later, you learn that your "ailment" coincided with the onset of a friend or family member's illness.

No one can lie to you because you can see through their facade and know what they really mean. You may even know whythey lied.

People-even strangers-open up and start volunteering their personal information. You may be sitting in the waiting room minding your own business and waiting your turn when the person next to you starts sharing all kinds of personal information. You didn't ask them to and they never considered that you might not want to hear about their drama. People may feel better after speaking with you, but you end up feeling worse because they have transferred their emotional pain to you.

Some empaths don't do well with intimate relationships. Constantly taking on their partner's pain and emotions, they may easily get their feelings hurt, desire to spend time alone rather than with the partner, feel vulnerable when having sex, and feel that they have to continually retrieve their own energy when it gets jumbled with that of their partner. They may be so afraid of becoming engulfed by another person that they close up emotionally just to survive.

The ill, the suffering, and those with weak boundaries are drawn to the unconditional understanding and compassion an empath emits without even being aware of it. Until you learn how to shut out the energy of others, you may have a pretty miserable existence in which you feel like you have to be entirely alone to survive.

It's easy to see why being an empath is often very draining. No wonder that over time, some folks shut down their empathic ability. And, with that, they also shut down a vital part of their divine guidance system. Learn how to manage the amount of info-energy you receive and hear more of what is really important.

An Empath is a person who was born with unique variations in the central nervous system. This means how the brain is configured and how the nervous system works in the body. This has not yet been studied and quantified by science. Instead it is being brought forth by individuals who are becoming self-aware of these qualities and who explore this experience through creative and intuitive outlets.

A high degree of overall sensitivity is the general indicator for this type of person. All of the sensory organs of an empath have low thresholds thereby resulting in unusual sensitivity to light, smell, and sound (as well as other subtler senses). Although underlying sensitiviy is the unifying factor behind all empaths, how this sensitivity is managed or funneled varies from person to person.

Chapter 2: Benefits of Being an Empath

Empaths are drawn to healing themselves and others. They are usually drawn to healing, because they feel that they have so much internal healing to do... until, that is, they realize that most of the healing needed is for others that they are intuitively 'feeling'.

Is it hard for you to see any benefit in being an empath? Do you feel being highly sensitive is a problem for you? Most people feel that their heightened awareness or sensitivity is a burden that they want it to shut off and quiet. It's really important for you to hear how valuable you are as an empath, and how many wonderful traits you have that set you apart and give you an advantage because you are highly sensitive.

When you get a better understanding of your true nature, realize you are not alone, start accepting your heightened sensitivities and then learn the practicable methods that will be shared with you, you will be able to gradually identify and release all those pesky internalized false beliefs you have about how there is something wrong with you.

What if what you believe is wrong about you was your greatest capacity for changing the world and you just don't yet know how to use your natural abilities yet?

As most of you, or maybe all of you have concluded at one time or another in life, being highly sensitive can be tough. You may feel like no one understands you and no one gives you the sympathy you require when something is difficult for you.

There are actually some great benefits of being highly empathic. Most people put all the focus on the difficulties and don't get far enough in their self-discovery on their own to realize the enormous benefits.

We are natural healers and can gift healing energy to others through our hands, voices or even by playing a musical instrument. Many empaths choose to pursue energy healing as they feel an inner calling to heal themselves and others.

The heightened sense of smell allows empaths to enjoy food, beverages, flowers, essential oils, etc. with more intensity. If you work to increase your skill of smell you can also smell death or disease in an animal or a person. This can lead to saving lives.

Empaths sense potential dangers before other people and are more in tune with their sixth sense.

Since they feel everything so strongly, they are prone to feeling deeper lows, but also are prone to feeling greater highs than those who are not as sensitive. Most have a great enthusiasm for life and experience live and joy with greater intensity and tend to be more kind, understanding, compassionate and caring.

While many people who are not so empathic feel deeply uncomfortable being alone with themselves, Empaths actually crave a lot of alone time and require it to balance and de-stress. They need alone time to recuperate, and that's not a bad thing as they are more self-aware because of this time with themselves.

Empaths are unusually very creative in life with not only art but also experiences, situations, and possibilities. They think differently and see things that others would not be able to conceptualize as easily.

This creativity of thought and processing can often be mislabeled as wrong, but it's actually a capacity of theirs.

They can read emotional cues and are very emotional themselves, so they can imagine well what the other person feels and what would happen inside if this person did not have their needs met.

Sensitive people are good at sensing all kinds of nonverbal communication and indicators of physical needs and emotions. This gives empaths a talent for intuiting the unconscious mind and for sensing the needs of those who cannot speak, such as animals, plants, infants, and the human body.

They also are much more aware of people's thoughts feelings and emotions, and because of this, they can almost always sense when someone is lying to them. They know when someone says they are fine, but they really are crying on the inside. Because if their heightened awareness they can see through the false facades people up.

People can not lie to empaths without them knowing. Even when someone tries to tell them they are ok but they are not, they see though the facade being put up, and can feel what's really going on under the surface.

Your heightened sensitivity is a gift and not a curse. Remember that your thoughts are things, and what you think is what you create. So, next time you curse your heightened awareness or sensitivity level remember some of these benefits that you've just uncovered.

By putting your focus on the benefits of being an empath, you will be creating a life where your gift is contributing to you instead of draining you.

Chapter 3: Awakening the Sleeping Empath Within You

To begin with you are already psychic. That means you are already receiving information through levels distinct from your ordinary senses of sight, smell, taste, touch, and hearing. Therefore, there is no actual need for you to develop "psychic abilities." If you practice "psychic development" exercises that is fine and it is your own choice but it can be a waste of time without perspective.

You may or may not have realized this part of yourself yet. Every person, and in fact, every living thing on this planet is psychic (and that essentially means that we are all "interconnected" on levels that are not readily apparent - yielding more information than we have currently acknowledged or understood.)

Specifically, Empaths have highly attuned sensitivity to the emotional and mental states of others, as a result of active psi abilities. Everyone has a psychic potential, but not everyone knows how to access or utilize that potential on a regular basis, in a useful way. Until this part of our brains is properly mapped out by science, most work in this area will be guess work. (speculation)

The primary venue for "psychic connection" occurs between people and living things, so psychic communication takes place primarily between people. Empaths are "psychic" about people; more so than about objects, times, or events. Therefore, the term Empath here indicates an active people focused psychic, a person who listens to and utilizes the silent language of Dreamtongue to enhance relationships and communications. In theory, an Empath should be an expert in relationships and communications.

Intuitive information is always present within your mind. You may not be aware of that information.

The problem or challenge is that intuitive information is largely received and stored in your unconscious. The way to tap into that information is by listening in to a very subtle dialog that is occurring in your head even as you read this. It is possible that you have many dialogs, voices, or thoughts going on in your mind at all times, drowning out the intuitive information available to you. This is the problem of the discursive mind. There is a exercise that tames this issue very effectively.

That internal dialog is the result of your conscious and unconscious communicating with each other in a continuous feedback loop. You may or may not have noticed this dialog before. Most of us notice the nagging, critical version of an inner voice that dissects our thoughts and feelings. Most of us are preoccupied with that voice. Yet there is a more powerful, more "REAL" voice just underneath all that inner mental noise.

It is a very small and soft "voice" or form of information, often referred to as the small still voice within.

That dream voice is the one that urges you at times to turn right on a street, to pick up the phone and call someone, or to avoid a certain place at a certain time. Often we ignore that voice and think later that we should have listened. It's more of a feeling than a sound, yet it is something somewhere in-between, an echo. That dream voice is the one that urges you at times to turn right on a street, to pick up the phone and call someone, or to avoid a certain place at a certain time. Often we ignore that voice and think later that we should have listened. It's more of a feeling than a sound, yet it is something somewhere in-between, an echo. We have a level of communication available to us that is not limited by time and space.

How often have you said something like, "I kept thinking that I should call you but I just didn't," or, "something kept telling me to drive down that street but I just thought I was being silly?"

This tiny little messenger comes from the feedback loop between your conscious and unconscious mind. It is difficult to listen to this voice because it speaks a different language, the empathic language of Dreamtongue. An important distinction between the "conscious mind voice" and the" unconscious mind voice" is as follows:

- ✓ The "conscious voice", the rational waking mind, speaks loud and clear. It's primary mode is to analyze, break things down, and utilize those things.
- ✓ The "unconscious mode," the intuitive subconscious mind, speaks in whispers, shades, and metaphors. Its primary mode is to synthesize, put together, and reveal more gestalt workings.

When the intuitive voice is trying to tell you something it is often a matter of guessing the message. It is very much like talking to someone who speaks a different language than you. Occasionally you can get the gist of what they are trying to say but it is mostly guess work.

This is where most of us struggle with intuitive nature. We are often aware that we are receiving or sensing some information but do not know how to interpret it. The dream voice comes from the sleeping empath within. This metaphor is the most appropriate to encourage a subjective feeling, like having a rosebud inside that has yet to bloom. The potential of awakening a sleeping empath within invites growth and transformation on many levels.

Your inner empath/psychic is sleeping because it is within your unconscious, its "eyes" are closed but it still sees, its ears are closed but it still hears. Your inner empath whispers to you when you are awake. It is your best friend and your guide. It is you, in your fullest capacity.

When you sleep you travel into your unconscious where the barrier between you and your inner empath disappears. In your sleep, you experience the language of your unconscious through dreams. Once you awaken that language fades into the background and becomes the quiet dream voice once again.

Chapter 4: The Basics of Empathic Language

Dreamtongue is the language of the unconscious, the language of dreams and the empathic levels of the mind. Here I want to give you working definitions of the terms conscious and unconscious. This is the foundation of the language.

The conscious mind is the part of you that uses words to think and to deal with information. The conscious mind involves all those things of which you are aware at any given moment. The normal flow of the conscious mind deals with sensory input from the eyes, ears, nose, taste buds, and sense of touch.

The conscious mind is synthesized from the verbal centers of the brain, the language centers. Any thought or perception organized by words, by language, and, of which you are aware, is occurring in your conscious mind.

Remember the analogy that your waking mind is the Sun? The Sun provides light and light is awareness. When you become aware of something it has entered your conscious mind.

The unconscious mind deals with information as well but does not directly use words. You process stimuli without words and it is this processing that I am referring to as the unconscious. It is still possible to receive information without being aware of it. The classic example is that you can be sitting in a room with a clock ticking and not be aware of the sound. Your ears still pick up the sound but you are not paying attention to it, therefore no thought is attached to it. In other words, it does not enter your conscious mind.

Another example might be that subtle shifts in temperature and motion occur when someone is walking up from behind you, but you are not consciously aware of that person. Your own body chemistry and nervous system may respond to those shifts but no thought is attached to them. You are then receiving information about a person coming up behind you but not from what you see or hear directly. This information is being processed through your unconscious mind, your nonverbal centers.

The potential for receiving information in this way is proprioception. Some people have used proprioception to explain away empathic abilities but in so doing they are throwing the baby out with the bathwater. Proprioception is just the tip of the iceberg, the tip of the unconscious mind.

The unconscious goes much deeper than proprioception. Anything that is occurring within your body is part of your unconscious. In fact, to truly understand and define the unconscious would be to say that your body itself is the unconscious!

You are all mind and all body. There is no separation from the two. Once you work with that understanding you will be amazed at how much empathic information has been knocking at your door, just waiting for you to open that door! The world of infinite possibilities opens up when you understand that mind and body are one thing.

Yet our language cuts the two in apart no matter how carefully we choose our words.

Just as the conscious mind links to the verbal centers of the brain, the unconscious links into the associational centers. The associational centers are more like the memory of things seen or the memory of things heard, rather than being involved with actual seeing and hearing.

Now this is important: the associational centers form the channel between the conscious mind and the unconscious mind. This is the place where the small still voice within originates. The dialogue inside of this channel is the dream voice, the place where Dreamtongue occurs.

To break these definitions of conscious and unconscious down into usable forms: The conscious mind communicates with words as language; the unconscious mind communicates with associations as language.

When you look at a decorated Christmas tree your senses tell you that it is a green tree with objects attached to it. It is probably not doing anything other than holding still and blinking with small lights. Yet, a deeper perception of the tree is occurring involving all types of feelings that are the result of associations.

When you look at a Christmas tree you do not just see a tree with objects on it, you see Christmas past and present, you have many feelings of all sorts, you associate it with all types of experiences.

Since you have probably had a lot of practice with responding to Christmas trees, most of your associations to the tree flow readily into your conscious mind. When you are not aware of those associations they remain dormant in your unconscious.

Empathic information, by definition, originates within your unconscious. It usually stays there unless it creates an impulse strong enough to surface in some fashion. Empathic information does not have the direct link to sight and hearing as does sensory information.

Sensory information communicates to you externally then is taken internally for processing. Empathic information works exactly the opposite. Empathic information originates internally and then can be communicated externally. Empathic information is by definition, always a response to something.

Too often people try to measure empathic information by the same standards as sensory information. It is equivalent to the fellow looking for his keys under the lamp because there is more light. It does not work to treat empathic information and sensory information as the same phenomenon. Therefore you cannot use the same instruments or procedures to measure them.

Dreamtongue is the language of the unconscious, the language of dreams, of symbols and associations, of archetypes, and the levels of empathic awareness. It is a language rich in meaning and impact on our lives. Normal verbal language is very limited by comparison.

Dreamtongue is like communicating in holograms. A hologram is a special type of photography that produces a three dimensional image. If the photographic plate is shattered into pieces, each piece is capable of producing the full three-dimensional image of the original. Each piece contains the essence of the whole.

Advanced theorists in science and philosophy have proposed that the universe itself is one singular hologram of which we are all a part. Each part then contains the essence of the whole. Dreamtongue speaks with symbols and associations that are in effect holograms. Any part of Dreamtongue contains the essence of every other part, so if you only get a tiny bit of information, that tiny bit contains the entire message. With all of this said, Dreamtongue is remarkably simple and beautiful.

There are five primary levels of empathic perception. These five levels constitute the "grammar" of Dreamtongue. Just as in verbal language there are nouns, verbs, adjectives, etc., in Dreamtongue there are betas, thetas, alphas, etc. Learning about these levels and the "mechanics" of the language will help you speak and interpret the language.

Yet it is not imperative that you memorize the structure and parts of Dreamtongue unless you want to teach Dreamtongue. Once you begin working with it you will find that it is a "living" force which empowers you naturally. It is your own natural language, coming from your heart, your soul, and all levels of your being.

The Five Levels of Dreamtongue

In normal language you learn parts of speech and the rules for using the language. First you learn the alphabet, then small words, then more words, and eventually how to put the words together.

Learning about the five levels of Dreamtongue is just like learning the empathic alphabet. The empathic alphabet is simpler because it only has five letters! These five letters also constitute a set of "grammar rules" for the flow of Dreamtongue.

Sounds incredible that such a powerful language has only five letters, but remember that the language is holographic. An entire message is available in one bit of information. To make the empathic alphabet usable by the conscious mind, Greek letters can be used to describe them.

The five letters of the empathic alphabet are (in order): Beta, Alpha, Theta, Delta, and Gamma. It is not important here to know the actual Greek letters for we are not talking normal written language. Remember Dreamtongue works by associations, not by literal definition.

Beta

When the brain is aroused and actively engaged in cognitive or mental activities, it generates beta waves. Beta waves are of relatively low amplitude, and are the fastest of the four different brainwaves. The frequency of beta waves ranges from 15 to 40 cycles a second.

When you are actively engaged in a conversation you are generating beta waves. A person delivering a passionate speech is in a high beta state. In Dreamtongue, Beta is your conscious waking state. The more active and alert you are the more Beta you generate. Beta is the mainframe for the software in your brain, in other words, the "foundation" for your conscious mind.

Alpha

Alpha brainwaves are slower and higher in amplitude. Their frequency ranges from 9 to 14 cycles per second. You are generating alphas when you relax, are near day dreaming, near sleep, or just entering sleep.

The most intense Alpha state is the hypnogogic state, which is right before you fall asleep. Alpha is fertile ground for empathic receptivity; it is the primary channel of empathic awareness.

Theta

Theta brainwaves, are typically of even greater amplitude and slower frequency than Alpha waves. This frequency range is normally between 5 and 8 cycles a second. You normally only generate thetas when you are in deep sleep or in the middle of a powerful meditation.

The R.E.M (rapid eye movement) stage of sleep and dreaming are associated with Theta. Theta is the inner screen upon which you view empathic information and imagery.

Delta

Delta brainwaves are of the greatest amplitude and slowest frequency. They typically range from 1.5 to 4 cycles per second. Typically, 2 to 3 cycles a second.

You generate deltas when you are in deep dreamless sleep, so deep that it would be difficult to wake you. It is also possible to generate deltas when you are in profound states of meditation and altered states of consciousness. Fully actualized and trained Empaths can generate a Delta state with their eyes open.

Gamma

Gamma is distinct from the above four states. Delta involves brain waves at 1 to 4 cycles per second. So it seems we have run out of brain waves doesn't it?

Gamma is not associated with specific brain wave states; rather it is the source state of consciousness. It is the potential for consciousness and the potential for any brain wave state. It is the holographic potential of the mind expressed as a unified field, the mental equivalent of "implicate order" a concept you will be introduced to in later lessons.

Gamma is the source of consciousness which eludes the microscope and the trained eye. You generate gamma simply by "being". Gamma is not identified in other systems, it is unique to Dreamtongue.

Beta is related to empathic activity expressed through the physical body and through physical objects. Beta events are psychokinesis, mind over matter, influence by thought, moving objects with the mind, etc.

What normally comes to mind with Beta events are images of someone willing the needle of a compass to move, or bending spoons, or the more dramatic idea of levitation. Yet psychokinesis or telekinesis is better understood through phenomenon like empathic healing.

The ability of your empathic mind to influence your own body and the body of another better captures the nature of Beta.

Alpha is related to general empathic sensitivity. The Alpha state is a more receptive state than Beta. Beta "generates," Alpha 'receives." In Beta the waking mind you are more in a state of generating or sending out signals. In the Alpha state, you are opening up your awareness to greater degrees of receptivity.

In Alpha you become more aware of internal signals and can better focus on your dream voice. You are tuning out some of the outside world and are listening in to the internal word of the unconscious.

The Alpha level relates to generalized types of empathic functioning like sensing emotions, sensing danger, unusual feelings that are "signals", general or vague intuition, hunches, and feelings in general are Alpha messages.

Theta is basically what you can call "psychic" central. It is the place where empathic information is processed. When you are asleep and dreaming a vivid dream you are in a Theta state and in that state empathic information is woven into the fabric of the dream.

Theta involves mind to mind communication, or telepathy. Telepathy is when two people speak Dreamtongue to each other at the Theta level. Telepathy is possible between all living things plant or animal. Telepathy involves the process of listening or empathic hearing.

It is not a matter of "reading another person's mind," which is more of a stage trick. It is the result of two or more nervous systems becoming synchronized or linked in some fashion. The communication can involve thinking the same or similar thoughts or having the same feelings, physical or emotional. Theta is the "point" where we connect with others.

Delta is the source of all the empathic information that is processed in Theta. Here information exists as holograms, composites, and gestalts. Delta is related to the very function of empathic perceiving. It is the level of empathic vision or "clairvoyance."

Here information comes as pictures, images, and symbols, all which contain information that can be translated into feelings, thoughts, and words. Delta is the sleeping Empath within you. Sleeping because it is shut off from the senses but very active and very powerful within your unconscious.

Gamma is the level that baffles everyone and even eludes the serious researchers of parapsychology. Gamma is the place beyond all of our senses and awareness. From Gamma comes perception of future and past events. It cannot be clearly defined nor can it be fully controlled.

The previous four levels of empathic functioning relate to the interconnectedness between living things. The abilities of precognition, seeing into the future, and retrocognition, seeing into the past, result from an understanding of existence that is not available to our conscious minds. Although a veritable universe of speculation exists in this area, you should keep an open mind with regards to explaining Gamma phenomenon.

At the Gamma level, we enter the world of metaphysical and spiritual knowledge, something that best communicated through Dreamtongue, through symbols, myths, archetypes, ideas, and associations. Dreamtongue involves at first a deep understanding and connection with Gamma, then in the advanced stages, it involves a very careful and deliberate use of words and images to evoke and process information.

All five levels of empathic functioning do not occur independently of each other. They are all happening at the same time within you right now. You learn them separately but eventually you merge your understanding of them all working in unison. The Delta state is active within you right now even though you are not in a deep sleep, but it is active in the unconscious.

Each part of your self communicates with every other part creating a continuous flow of dreamtongue.

Chapter 5: Developing Empathic Awareness

Beta is the first level of the empathic language. This stage introduces you to plugging your five primary senses into available empathic information. Remember the sleeping empathic within you is functionally separate from your conscious mind and does not normally use your primary senses. To the empathic within you, Beta is the outer world, the surface world, the outermost regions of your psyche.

For all practical purposes, Beta is everything that is perceived by your eyes, ears, nose, taste buds, touch, etc. You are in a Beta state when you are awake and alert. A Beta state occurs as you are generating an abundance of brain wave cycles per second. The more active you are the more brain waves you can generate.

You might want to call Beta the "nonempathic" level, but don't. There is no such thing as a nonempathic level. Empathic phenomenon occurs because of an innate connectedness between all things, especially living things. Due to the fact that your primary senses are active in Beta, your brain has been conditioned to rely on those senses for survival.

Your primary senses are your outermost senses but they, too, have deep roots in the unconscious. Through the Beta stage, you will learn to use what your outermost senses provide in order to interpret empathic information.

Beta is you as a whole solid entity with mass, density, weight, etc. The empathic part of Beta is actually your eyes, ears, nose, etc.; empathic because these organs take signals in to your interior world, your psyche. They are essentially gateways to your inner world. These gateways are limited by their physical dimensions but are very practical tools.

The limitation of those senses is represented by the yellow square of Beta. The yellow is light, awareness, boxed in on four sides. The four sides indicate an orientation to the physical world by representing north, south, east, and west in their respective places.

All of this information sounds very fundamental and elementary – and it is. But if you make an effort to learn it you will be prepared for more complex courses that provide truly amazing insight into empathic functioning.

Since information from the primary senses is dominant at the Beta level for most people, information from the innermost senses hides behind the conscious mind. As you will learn, the innermost senses are Alpha, Theta, and Delta. The omniscient Gamma mind, which you possess, cannot really be described as a sense.

At the Beta level information from your primary senses floods your brain on a continuous basis, keeping your awareness busy most of the time. Direct empathic information, information that is not apparent to your primary senses, is typically drowned out by all the activity in your waking mind. All the activity in your waking mind is a form of "mental noise," which is almost always louder than your dream voice. The dream voice is always present and always available.

Your dream voice is simply your empathic awareness at the Beta level. It is the connecting point between your innermost and outermost senses. Beta is then, the vehicle for the entire process. This makes Beta VERY important: not something to avoid, skirt around, or ignore. Instead Beta is your key to powerful empathic functioning.

Beta is the vehicle for the entire empathic process and that vehicle is your full body/mind system. Beta is the receiver and the sender of information. The Beta senses are constrained by physical limitations but are rooted in the deeper senses, which have no physical constraints.

Your body is your Beta level. Your waking mind is your Beta level. Other than empathic dreaming, much of your empathic work will occur while you are in Beta, or are awake. To become an active empathic, you must connect your normal waking state with your empathic nature. You do this by understanding the nature of Beta and by understanding that empathic information is available through sensory information.

To understand how empathic information is available through sensory information requires rethinking some more beliefs about empathic abilities.

At the Beta stage, it is important to be alert, aware, and observant. The greater your ability to concentrate and focus, the greater your mastery of Beta will be. Pay attention to details without getting hung up on them. Take in your environment with open awareness. The more you are aware of what you see, hear, smell, and touch, the more you will be able to link your senses to your empathic awareness.

Don't wait for some mysterious message or feeling to emerge in order to retrieve empathic information. Simply look around you. Feel the environment around you with your eyes. Do not put sensory information in a category separate from empathic information. It is all one and the same, it's all information. Empathic information can be enhanced by sensory information and sensory information can be enhanced by empathic information.

At times sensory information and imagination act as a form of mental noise that makes it hard for the beginning empath to process empathic information. Strong emotional states can interfere with empathic reception. Imagined fears and intense desires are also at work within your psyche.

Beta relates to empathic activity expressed through the physical body. Not only through the physical senses but also through physical states. These states can be electrical, chemical, or nuclear.

Empathic energy or internally generated energy (innergy) is always present within you. This energy can impact your physical, emotional, and mental state. It can also impact the physical, emotional, and mental state of another person.

Whenever you extend your empathic energy outside of yourself to another person or an object, this activity is called psychokinesis or telekinesis. Psychokinesis is intentionally sent Beta energy. The origin of that intent can be either conscious or unconscious.

Unfortunately, movies and television have imprinted on most people the image of psychokinesis (PK) as lifting large objects with the mind and flinging them across a room. The dramatic portrayals of PK as superhuman and supernatural make it seem to be the most unlikely of all empathic abilities. Yet it is very human and very accessible by anyone.

The best application for PK is through what has been popularly called empathic healing. If you concentrate on another person you can send your own empathic energy to that person. There are many people in the world who have devoted themselves to the idea of healing and helping others. They have trained and conditioned their empathic energy to work with thoughts of repair, regeneration, healing, love, and compassion.

When a healing empath concentrates on another person she is sending Beta messages of healing, love, and compassion. For a healer to do this, their own body fills up with the healing energy, their Beta state, with energy of love, healing, and compassion until it over flows and transfers to another person. Which leads to another important point.

Can empathic energy be used to generate harm or negativity? First, look at how the process works. The sender would have to first fill up with harmful and negative energy until it overflowed. They would then have to be capable of directing that energy to another person while consumed with the negativity.

Who would be the first victim of such an attack? You guessed it, the sender. It is not impossible but the sender pays a great cost and is consumed by the energy before being able to send it.

Generating a Beta Message

To generate a Beta message simply requires an action. Every action you take, no matter how small, generates a Beta message. Your physical presence in a room generates a Beta message. Beta energy is something you generate all the time to move your body.

You can learn to generate Beta energy in more creative ways. Symbolic gestures associated with specific intent can be very powerful Beta messages. For example, each time you want to send healing energy you can touch your heart with your hands as you focus on the target of your healing. Some people like to touch their forehead as they concentrate on receiving empathic information. The classic images of witches and magicians gesturing with specific intent certainly comes to mind when considering ways to generate Beta messages.

Observe your body language and expressive gestures to see how you are already performing this empathic act. The type of gestures and movements you associate with specific empathic functions should be unique and meaningful to you personally. With practice, you will find creative and meaningful movements which will evolve from your own empathic practice.

Beta is the foundation for creative action or "ritual." Hand gestures, for example, are Beta messages. If your hand gesture contains within it an Alpha message, or association, regarding relaxation and calm, then you can send Beta energy to calm and relax someone.

Creative actions or rituals generate a theme of Beta messages for specific goals: healing, restoring, protecting, connecting, celebrating, sharing, etc. For example, an empathic healer moving his or her hands over the area around someone's body to generate healing energy, is what is meant by ritual. The moving around of the hands is not really necessary but it acts as a Beta channel.

most exciting action you can take to send a Beta message is one we normally take for granted: The act of talking generates Beta messages. The power of the human voice carries Beta signals. This also works the other way around. When someone is talking to you they are sending you Beta messages.

Last, but definitely not least, what you could call the "most empathic" level of Beta. It is only the "most empathic" level in the traditional sense of what we think of as empathic or even "psychic". Since Beta is essentially your body/mind, messages that originate from within your unconscious, from the inner empathic, are felt within your body. This form of Beta message takes the form of physical sensations and changes. Empaths are all about feeling: not just emotionally but through physical states as well.

These Beta messages can be through: an increase or decrease in body temperature, an increase or decrease in physical tension (such as around the stomach area), specific sensations on the skin, tingling or pain in the body, an increase or decrease in sense of weightiness (suddenly feeling heavier and slower, or feeling lighter and faster), and so on.

Beta is the level of "gut reactions," bodily responses to empathic perceptions. You may not be consciously aware of what your body is responding to at first.

Areas of empathic sensitivity vary from person to person, but common areas for Beta body messages are the

- ✓ temples & forehead,
- ✓ the back of the neck,
- ✓ the throat,
- ✓ the chest,
- ✓ and the stomach.

Pretty much down the center of the body following the path of the spine. The spine carries the central nervous system down from the brain to the rest of the body and serves as the pathway for empathic information.

Some empathic traditions of yoga have identified seven empathic centers in the spine. These seven centers have been called "chakras." The way people tend to receive Beta body messages along the center of the body appears to correlate fairly well with the idea of the seven empathic centers.

Chapter 6: Developing Empathic Sensitivity

Alpha is the internal world of your psyche. It is the place of dreams, imagery, memory, myth, emotion, and shadows. Where Beta is the bright yellow light of the Sun enclosed by the four sides of a square,

Alpha is the light reflected from the surface of the Moon, symbolized in a silver crescent. The silver crescent is an excellent symbol for Alpha the unconscious.

The Moon reflects the light of the Sun but is covered in partial darkness from a shadow. The partial Moon light of the crescent represents the partial consciousness of Alpha and the shadow over the Moon suggests the presence of the unconscious.

An Alpha state occurs when you slow your brain waves down to around 8 to 13 cycles per second. This can be done by closing your eyes and relaxing. Visualizing a peaceful scene and taking a few deep breaths will take you even deeper into Alpha. Alpha is just under the surface of your waking mind and is always available to you.

A common, yet outdated, term for Empathic ability is "the sixth sense." This implies one more sense past the five primary senses. In fact, we really have more than five primary senses. In addition to sight, hearing, touch, taste, and smell, we have a kinesthetic sense which detects movement and body orientation.

There are even subtler senses within the body. All of these senses form a ladder that extends down into the unconscious levels of the mind. For now, I will keep the primary senses lumped into the first five of Beta and refer to Alpha as the sixth sense.

Alpha as the sixth sense acts like a compass or divining rod within your body/mind. It generates vague or undefined information that can create a sense of a push or a pull within you. A pull would be a desire to move toward something, a push would be a reaction to move back from something or someone.

In the language of Dreamtongue Alphas are hunches, intuitions, general feelings, inclinations, unexplained reactions/responses. If an Alpha message is strong enough it will push its way up (or out) through the body and become a Beta message.

Whether an empathic message is heard as an Alpha or a Beta depends upon two things:

- ✓ You as an individual. Are you more aware of your feelings or your body states, or both?
- ✓ The intensity and importance of the message.

You are continuously receiving Alpha messages throughout your day. Not all of them are important enough to signal you through your body, unless you are an extremely sensitive to your body states. If you are a person who tends to not really pay attention to your body states or feelings, then you may not be noticing Alpha or Beta messages.

Have you ever walked in to a place and thought, "I have a bad feeling about this?", or, " I have a good feeling about this?" If so, then you were acknowledging an Alpha message.

Alpha is the level of Empathic impressions. These impressions are usually not very clear or distinctive and therefore require interpretation. It is in the process of interpreting Empathic impressions that many people lose the message or reach inaccurate conclusions.

Alpha is also the "emotional level," in the same way that Beta is the "physical level." Empathic messages come in through emotional responses. The distinction between a normal emotional reaction and an Alpha message depends on what is occurring around you.

If you get upset because someone is yelling at you then that is a normal emotional reaction. If you think of something upsetting and then you get upset, that is a normal emotional reaction. If you are talking to friend and enjoying yourself, and then for no apparent reason you get upset - that could be an Alpha message.

The Alpha level relates to overall empathic sensitivity. Learning about the nature of empathic sensitivity will help anyone who feels they have trouble accessing Empathic information.

Normal sensitivity is measured in thresholds. Sensitivity to touch, to temperature, and to pain is measured by how much of each stimulus is needed before a person can feel that stimulus. The point where there is enough pressure or stimulation to feel the touch, heat, pain, etc., is the threshold.

Alpha messages originate from within you due to some distant or unapparent stimulation or pressure. The amount of "internal pressure" required in order for you to recognize an empathic message is your Alpha threshold. It is your Alpha threshold that determines your level of Empathic sensitivity. This threshold varies throughout the day and can vary from day to day.

Empathic sensitivity can be developed as a skill. You can expand your Alpha threshold which, in turn, increases your Empathic sensitivity. This is the essence of stage four of your training. To expand your Empathic sensitivity you must first learn how to compare Alpha with Beta states.

Beta and Alpha act as mirror images of each other. They are like the Sun and the Moon, with the Moon reflecting the light of the Sun. Beta takes signals in to your body/mind and Alpha receives signals internally from within your unconscious. Beta information is encoded by your senses but Alpha is information not perceived by your senses.

The lack of sensory input is what makes Alpha messages difficult to recognize and interpret. If you cannot see it, hear it, or touch it, how can you know what it is? What is missing is the means for the Alpha message to get encoded into some usable form. Alpha messages are encoded by associations.

Alpha is the whisper of your dream voice. Alpha messages are harnessed by forming associations to other information, especially symbolic imagery.

Forming associations to Empathic impressions is the key skill of the empath. When an Alpha message arises within you and you do not immediately recognize it's purpose, you can make associations with it and discover its meaning. This is done much like the process of what is called "free association." Free association works by having someone present words to you one at a time and you say whatever comes to mind without censoring.

Here are the guidelines for developing your Empathic sensitivity by practicing Alpha associations.

Alpha Associating Exercise

✓ Sit in a comfortable position so that you are reasonably relaxed. Remember, relaxing slows down your brain to an Alpha level.

✓ Focus on an object or person. If the object or person is in front of you, then you look at the target without paying attention to details. You simply take in the overall image without focusing on a specific part of the target. Remember you are not looking for information with your eyes. Some people prefer to close their eyes during this part but that is a matter of personal preference. You can even hold an object in your hand to practice associating. When you Alpha associate while holding or touching something it is called "psychometry."

✓ Allow thoughts, words, pictures, etc. to come to mind without censoring them. Do not decide which thoughts are Empathic and which ones are not. If you do that, then you are censoring and that impedes the process. Just let whatever pops into your mind to come forward. The skill of Alpha associating develops by actually speaking the associations out loud or by writing them down. To keep from being slowed down you might want to use a tape recorder or have someone write your associations down.

- ✓ The "knack" or skill comes by catching the very first impressions, the more immediate the associations the better. Any time spent on analyzing or judging the associations cuts off the Alpha message. Receiving and interpreting Empathic information are two different functions. For the beginner it is very difficult to perform these two functions at the same time. For the sake of practice, do your receiving and your interpreting separately. Do not strain to "get" information. Empathic information is immediate. It's already there. Your only work is to retrieve it.
- ✓ Do not spend too long on any one target. Do your focusing and associating for a period of five to ten minutes at the very most.
- ✓ After you are done associating then review your list of impressions. It is at this point that you can evaluate or analyze the information for content. If there is no empathic content then do not worry, the purpose of the exercise is to develop the skill of Alpha associating. When there is an empathic message that needs to come through then this skill will be invaluable.

You are successful with Alpha associating when you allow impressions to form without censoring them. As you increase your ability to make Alpha associations your empathic sensitivity increases. Your empathic sensitivity is measured by the extent of your ability to make Alpha associations.

Alpha messages normally come to you when there is a need for you to know something. That need is determined by your interest in the information and the seriousness of the information. If someone you know really wants or needs to get in touch with you, their feelings will generate a Beta message (remember: empathic energy generated and sent out is a form of Beta).

Your reception of that message can occur at any level. If the person sending you the signal is in distress, then you might receive the message at a Beta level, with a physical reaction - let's say, a constriction in the chest. If the signal is not that strong, the emotions are not that intense, then you might receive the message at the Alpha level. As an Alpha message it might come as a vague feeling of "something you need to do," or a general feeling that pulls you in the direction of that person.

Chapter 7: Connecting To Your Inner Empath

Dreamtongue passes into your being and resonates deep within your psyche. You generate the empath language at all times, it flows from your center out through your mind/body into the world around you. To communicate with Dreamtongue requires that you look at life with the "eyes of an empath."

All of life is a language. Every living thing, every event and action, every object in existence is a part of that language. The movement and the relationship between every single thing are the silent words of Dreamtongue. You hear this language with your heart, speak it with your soul, and your thoughts can be the channel between the two.

Theta is the channel between your innermost empath sense and your outermost awareness. Whether or not Theta will someday be identified with a specific organ in the brain, like the pineal gland, the hippocampus, or the hypothalamus or if it remains simply as a "construct", is not important to your training as an empath.

It will eventually happen that science will "discover" empath abilities and will link them to specific parts of the brain. It is projected that empath abilities will be related to every part of the brain but will be specifically connected to the brain stem area, the amygdala, and the limbic system; areas that are tied into emotional responses, as well as general body responses. To become an empath only requires that you are aware of your empath center.

Theta awareness is deeper within your body/mind than Beta and Alpha, it is in your unconscious mind. Beta is your waking state, Alpha takes place just below your waking state, but Theta is normally only available to you during sleep. In Theta your brain waves slow way down to around 4 to 7 cycles per second.

You can consciously reach Theta through a profound meditational state with discipline and practice.

Theta is the level of vivid dreaming. When you are asleep and in a Theta state, R.E.M. (rapid eye movement) occurs as you dream. In Theta your body/mind takes everything that is going on within it and uses that material to produce a dream.

Dreams are the result of physiological states, mental and emotional states, memories, imagination, and empathic states. All of these states weave together into a tapestry we call dreams. Some dreams occur at the Alpha level and have that Alpha vagueness about them. Alpha dreams are general feelings and reactions, indistinct images, etc. Theta dreams are typically the vivid dreams that seem very real and colorful.

Dream research shows that everyone dreams every night and that all dreams are typically in color. The problem for some people is that they do not remember their dreams and/or do not remember the color. Memory of dreaming or the colors in the dream are often lost by the time a person wakes up. The place where this dream activity occurs is the Theta level.

Theta is the level where inner impressions and activities form into composite images and ideas. It is in Theta where the more defined empathic messages are available. A Theta message usually occurs as a thought that enters your awareness. "Oh, I need to call John," or "The phone is going to ring," or "This person is from Arkansas." Theta messages are basically specific by design. Specific in this context does not mean exact. By specific, it means that there is more content to the message than just a general feeling.

Theta is the level of telepathy, for lack of a better word. The working definition for telepathy is mind-to-mind communication. Telepathy occurs as two living things link up with each other at an empathic or unconscious level. Telepathy does not mean that you are reading a person's mind, like reading a ticker tape print out. There can be word for word communication but the more common type of telepathy involves just getting the same emotions and overall ideas of another person.

The sender of the message (either intentional or unintentional) may be thinking of you but not know how to reach you. You, as the receiver of the message may get a body sensation as a response to that message but would probably not notice it; you might get an Alpha response but it could be too vague to understand, if the message is persistent and you are paying attention, then you may have a Theta response in the form of a thought, "I need to call John." This whole process involves a telepathic connection but is not called telepathy until the thought occurs which encodes the message.

Telepathy includes the sending as well as the receiving of messages. As an empath, you will learn to do both. How well you send or receive depends a lot on your personality. A person who is a good listener and is sensitive to the feelings of others tends to be a good receiver. A person who is easily distracted and is not really interested in other people's thoughts and feelings generally has difficulty receiving.

When a person is self-absorbed they have difficulty receiving. At any given moment when you are exclusively focused on one thing or activity, you may not notice a telepathic message. Sending a telepathic message only requires that you think of the person you are sending it to while you focus on the thought. The more connected you feel to the person while you are sending the thought, the more direct the message will be.

The type of relationship you have with the sender/receiver also determines the quality of the telepathy. The closer you are to someone emotionally the greater your telepathic connections. If you feel comfortable being close to someone, you are more likely to experience a telepathic connection with that person. That is why if strangers asks you to "be telepathic" with them, the connection may be elusive as you may not be comfortable being so intimate with a stranger.

Telepathic connections are very intimate. This is why you always hear of mothers detecting their child in distress or lovers doing the same. If a stranger comes up to you and asks you to read their mind, there is very little connection between the two of you for any telepathy to occur. Empath abilities work by their own natural laws and understanding these laws will help you to function as an empath. Theta messages are determined by the strength and quality of the relationship between two or more people

Theta messages have content that is specific but not always exact. Since Theta messages originate from within your unconscious without the benefit of the eyes or ears they are not encoded into clear signals. The empath mind encodes them with the associations you form, either consciously or unconsciously.

The big difference between Alpha and Theta comes with how associations are made. In Alpha you learn to make empath associations consciously. In Theta the associations are already made at an unconscious level that rise up to the conscious mind. Your unconscious encodes the message using whatever materials are available to it, just like it does when you are dreaming. Functioning in a pure empath state, Theta is like dreaming while you are awake.

Your unconscious tends to be very creative when encoding information. It relies on symbology, analogy, myth, beliefs, perceptions, feelings, memories, imagination, ideas, and even special effects, in order to paint a Theta message for you. Imagery that is symbolic rather than actual is Theta imagery.

Theta is the level where empath impressions are encoded and the place where telepathy is processed. In Alpha the dream voice is heard as a faint and distant whisper. Theta is the dream voice, the voice of your inner empath. In Beta, the dream voice is not heard at all, only felt through the body. In Alpha the dream voice is faint and often drowned out by the mental noise of Beta. In a pure Theta state the voice would be loud and clear. The problem for you and me is that we are normally trying to hear the dream voice while awake, in a Beta or Alpha state. What is needed is a stronger connection to the inner empath

There are two methods you can use to strengthen your connection to Theta: reducing mental noise and using an "empath totem."

First, let's look at mental noise and how to manage it. "Manage" because you will never completely get rid of mental noise. Mental noise is all of the activity of your waking mind. It is every conscious thought, perception, feeling, and reaction what is going on at the Beta level. Mental noise is generally very loud and distracting in contrast with the quiet soft nature of your dream voice. Mental noise can be any or all of the following:

✓ What you are actively seeing, hearing, touching, smelling, and tasting at any given moment creates mental noise. If you are trying to listen to your dream voice and someone is revving up a motorcycle outside your window, that sound creates a lot of mental noise from your reaction to it. Until you learn to follow these Beta signals down to deeper levels, they tend to be very distracting and drown out the dream voice of Theta.

✓ Your conscious thoughts act as mental noise. When you are analyzing, judging, evaluating, and trying to interpret information, this creates mental noise. Critical thoughts are mental noise. Self-criticism is the most oppressive form of mental noise. Thoughts of "I can't do this," " This is pointless," "This is something only other people can do," are the most distracting forms of mental noise.

✓ Imagined impressions are also mental noise. Imagination is very useful in empathic functioning because it serves as an endless reservoir of imagery. Through imagination you are able to make Alpha associations, which is a way to mentally feel around in the unconscious, searching for empath content. Imagination is material that is fashioned by your psyche. Anything fashioned by your imagination has the potential to encode empath content. Do not be afraid of imagination, it is not the nemesis of empath evidence. Imagination is a powerful ability that can be utilized in many ways. Still, imagination can also generate mental noise. When your imagination generates images that do not have empath content, then it is mental noise.

✓ Memories can also act as mental noise. Remembered impressions can interfere with empathic impressions. If you are empathically trying to determine what to get a loved one as a gift, and the memory of all the things you've gotten before, or the memory of things they've told you keeps popping up, this acts as mental noise which drowns out the empathic information available through Theta.

Typically these four types of mental noise are all happening together in one big mesh of mental distraction. The Beta mind is a busy place with heavy traffic. The next important skill for an empath is to learn how to manage mental noise.

Managing Mental Noise

Apart from practicing overall stress management, taking good care of yourself, and having private time to reflect on your life, the best way to manage mental noise is to create a conditioned relaxation response within yourself.

There are many advanced ways of creating a relaxation response within yourself.

✓ Set aside 10 to 20 minutes a day for empath breathing.

- ✓ Be consistent and do not skip days. Under even the worst conditions you can squeeze in 5 minutes for the exercise.
- ✓ Practice the exercise when you are awake and alert. Do not do it right before going to sleep or within the first fifteen minutes of waking up.
- ✓ Practice the exercise where you feel you have enough privacy and with the least amount of distraction. Do not try this exercise with the television on or where you can hear human voices. Hearing people talking is very distracting.
- ✓ Sit in a comfortable position where you can hold your spine erect. Do not strain or sit stiffly. Make sure pillows support you (or a chair) and that you feel stable before you begin.
- ✓ The exercise is very simple; it involves counting your inhalations and your exhalations. Learning empathic breathing prepares you to learn the focused sitting meditation. Your first goal is to be able to do three sets of ten breaths. When you first start this you may not be able to do all of the breaths in perfect order. You will build up to this in time. Do not strain or do anything that makes you feel uncomfortable. Relax and breathe normally between breaths when you need to.
- ✓ Your second goal is to be able to take long slow breaths that start in the diaphragm and fill up to your chest. This inhalation is then held to the count of four and is followed by a long slow exhalation.

✓ The first breath begins by inhaling slowly through your nostrils, filling your lungs from the "bottom up." Fill up your lungs without straining. When your lungs are full then hold the breath to the count of four. Exhale slowly by pursing your lips and blowing out a long silent whistle. Empty your lungs as much as possible without straining. When your lungs are empty hold to the count of four again. This counts as one breath.

✓ Repeat for up to ten breaths. Controlling and counting the breaths develops the concentration and focus that you need in order to manage mental noise. When you first do this you may only be able to do one set of ten breaths. You may not even be able to do ten breaths, so do what you can. Whatever you do will start to work for you. It is important that you do not do anything that will make you uncomfortable. The idea is to relax and work with your breathing. Your breathing becomes something you are creating and refining. Each time you sit you work on improving your breathing and learning to relax into the experience.

✓ Your eventual goal is to perform three full sets of ten breaths. You can do more sets if it suits your capacity. As you do your sets count your breaths and keep your thoughts focused on the count. Other thoughts and images will come into your mind, simply let them be. Do not try to do anything with those thoughts and images.

✓ Sometimes you will find yourself traveling through different states of consciousness while you do this. Other times you will stay in a Beta state throughout the exercise.

Empath breathing is one of the best things you can do for yourself for many reasons. It will help you learn to manage your mental noise and it will help you increase your overall energy level as well. After you have practiced empathic breathing for a period of time, which differs from person to person, you will be able to turn down the mental noise in your head by taking ten breaths and counting each one.

Empath Totems

Another way to strengthen the connection to your inner empath is to work with an empath totem. An empath totem is a symbol that you choose to represent your own empath nature. It can be in any form you select with no limits. It is only important that the symbol have meaning and connection for you. It becomes your logo as an empath. In the same way that European families had family shields and crests representing their lineage, an empath can establish a totem to represent their particular link to the empath levels.

An empath totem is formulated at the Theta level, using symbology and association. Yet all levels of the empath are incorporated into the totem. To choose a totem simply requires that it be the one you desire, you feel connected to, that has meaning for you, and that it feels right.

Totems can evolve, change, grow, diversify, and transform. Whatever totem you choose now for your empath training will go through many stages of development as you grow in your life. The totem acts as a mirror of sorts reflecting the obvious and hidden parts of your psyche. It grows and changes as you grow and change. It becomes the connection to your empath self and acts as an extension of you. It is one of the most beautiful and powerful of the tools available to Empaths. Many fascinating uses and experiences with totems have been shared with me over the years.

A totem does not need to be secret but it does need to be sacred or special. It is a tool that is empowered when you treat it with respect and with purpose. It can be an abstract symbol, it can be a traditional symbol; it can be represented by an animal - real or "imaginary," It can be mythological or entirely created by your imagination. It will be the vessel into which your empath nature will flow. A totem acts as a tangible or visible connector to your essentially invisible empathic nature.

Select a totem in your time. You may already have one in mind or you may need to work on it for a while. You may be drawn to a totem by an Alpha or Beta message, or it may come to you through a dream. Once you have selected your totem you can begin to take steps to externalize it. You can externalize your totem in different ways. You can obtain pictures that have your totem in them. You can obtain objects, jewelry, and decorations of your totem.

You can create your totem through any type of medium you desire. After a while, your totem will take on a life of it's own directed by and connected with your empath nature. Eventually you will be able to retrieve empath impressions through your totem. In this capacity your totem can act as a Guide. Just having a totem acts as a grounding mechanism for your empath nature, energizing you and reinforcing the connection with your Theta level.

Chapter 8: Developing the Eyes of an Empath

Delta is the deepest level of measurable consciousness. You generate Delta brainwaves, which cycle between 1 to 4 per second, when you are in a deep profound sleep. It is also possible to enter a pure Delta state through profound states of meditation and deep states of trance. If your consciousness were an ocean then Delta would be the current just above the ocean floor.

Delta is the core of Theta, it is the "place" of the sleeping empath. The circle of Delta is like an egg or a seed containing the fullness of your empathic nature. Delta is what is nurtured by the practice of empathic breathing and the use of an empathic totem. Through empath training you fertilize and gestate Delta, like an egg to be hatched. In time, the egg opens and the inner empathic emerges within you and begins to grow within you like a fresh new life.

Delta is the fourth letter of the empathic alphabet and the fourth level of empathic functioning. At the Delta level empathic information is processed through inner vision by what was traditionally called, "clairvoyance," which means clear seeing.

Now this inner vision is often referred to as "remote viewing." It is the ability to see images within your mind without the benefit of your eyes. All functions of visualization and the use of imagery originate in Delta.

In Theta images drawn from the Delta level are used symbolically. For example the symbolic image of a tree may emerge as an empathic impression. The tree may represent the overall life of a person. If the tree is full of leaves and fruit, the empathic impression would be one of abundance, prosperity, health, and happiness. If the tree is bare it may indicate lack or unhappiness. It would depend on the associations you make while you focus on the image of the tree. If you see one of the branches breaking off the tree it could mean that someone or something is leaving, or a loss of some sort. The imagery of Theta is typically symbolic in this way.

In Delta the function of "remote viewing" involves more of an actual perception of images. A Delta message of a tree would be the image of an actual tree somewhere. A Theta message of a tree would be the symbolic use of the image. How do you tell the two apart? The answer is: by intent. The image of a tree originates in Delta because all imagery originates in Delta.

Delta images are either fashioned by imagination, memory, or by remote viewing. How you use the imagery is up to you. If you decide in your mind to use an image as a symbolic focus for empathic information, then that image will respond to your attention in a symbolic way. It is, after all, your mind and your thoughts.

All the images of inner vision are technically symbolic since they do not originate with the eyes directly. If your intent is to see a person or place through remote viewing, then that intent will guide the process. For the most part, symbolic and actual imagery overlap since the empathic mind works with gestalts, or holograms.

Visualizing occurs in degrees. Just thinking about an object is a form of visualizing. Right now, as you read this, think of a red delicious apple. Just by reading the words "red delicious apple" you immediately start to form impressions. Even if you did not immediately see the red apple in your mind, you at least started thinking about it.

Now try to picture the apple, not just the shiny red outside, but imagine yourself biting into the apple. Think about the crisp texture, the sweet flavor, and the delicious juice. Think about the contrast between the shiny red peel on the outside and the white crispy wetness inside. Think about the soft wafting scent of the apple.

Which of any of these images did you respond to the most? If you responded to any or all of them then you have been visualizing.

To get a sense of how you visualize, do the following simple exercise.

✓ First close your eyes and imagine that you are at home in your bedroom (unless you really are in your bedroom, in that case choose another equally familiar room). Then try to picture the room: try to see the bed, the furniture, any wall hangings, etc. You may have more response to picturing familiar objects like those in your bedroom. They are not really like actual photographs with vivid color and sharpness, are they? Visualize yourself moving around the room observing colors, shapes, objects, etc.

✓ Do this for about five minutes then open your eyes again. Notice the quality of these "images." They tend to be only remotely visual. You are not using your eyes to see these images; you are using memory and imagination to create images. If you have ever daydreamed or let your mind "wander" off to distant thoughts, then you were visualizing. The very process of thinking is a form of visualizing. You are thinking and visualizing all the time. By focusing your thoughts into one area you can bring a visualized picture into your mind.

The good news is that the practice of empathic breathing will also enhance your ability to visualize. As you do your breathing sessions you will notice images coming and going within your mind. As you progress, these images will become clearer and more abundant. Part of this involves learning to relax. The more relaxed you become the easier it is to visualize. When you are tense and breathing shallow it is more difficult to visualize.

The other good news is that your empathic totem is ready and waiting to improve your visualization skills! As you do your empathic breathing exercise, begin to incorporate your totem into the practice. You have probably done this already. As you are counting your breaths you can picture your totem in your mind. Do not try to force the image of your totem, just be aware of your totem and let any images of it appear. Record these experiences in your Dreamtongue journal.

You can also "talk" an image. You may receive a Delta message about a specific place; let's say a zoo. Someone wants you to meet him or her at the zoo but they cannot reach you by phone. At the Delta level, you get a mental picture of the zoo but you do not see the image in your mind. You may notice this message at the Beta level through a body signal, or at the Alpha level with a general feelings, or at the Theta level with thoughts and symbols.

The thoughts at the Theta level may be of animals or of an animal. You might start thinking about giraffes for no apparent reason. You are in the grocery store looking at broccoli when suddenly the thought of a giraffe occurs to you. You ask yourself, "Why am I thinking about a giraffe?" The picture of a giraffe may not be in your mind but the thought or word is there.

In thinking about an image you are talking the image, which often leads to the picture itself. At that point a picture of your friend standing at the zoo gate could form. From there associations may follow where you connect with the idea of the zoo and eventually the person.

The Looking Ahead Delta (L.A.D.) Exercise

Athletes do laps, Empaths do LAD's. The purpose of this exercise is twofold. First, the Looking Ahead Delta exercise helps you begin to practically develop your visualization skills. Second, the L.A.D. exercise trains your Delta level to work with your conscious Beta level. This is the pulling the rope to bring up your inner empathic from the depths. This is an exercise that you can do throughout your day without taking out any more time from your schedule.

A L.A.D. consists of visualizing something before it happens or before you know about it. For example, before you check your mailbox, visualize what is inside.

Other types of L.A.D. possibilities:

- ✓ Before you open a package visualize what is inside.
- ✓ Before you enter a room, visualize who and/or what is inside.
- ✓ Before calling someone, visualize what he or she is doing.
- ✓ Before taking a walk, visualize what you might see.

Do this two to three times a day or as often as you like. Do it in ways that are comfortable and convenient for you. Do not push it or become too concerned with it. This is an exercise that needs to be fun and relaxed. Straining too hard to do a L.A.D. exercise works to the opposite effect, by closing off the Delta channel. When you first start you will have to remind yourself to practice. Eventually it will become second nature, where you will form mental pictures ahead of an event.

Here is the key to this exercise: in the same way that Alpha Associating is practiced without concern over empathic content, L.A.D.'s are performed without concern about empathic images. The purpose of the exercise is to train your Delta awareness to become a conscious function. In time the strength you develop in your Delta level will be useful for remote viewing.

It is the same as in weight lifting. After you lift weights you do not instantly get the full desired physique. After steady work for a length of time you end up with the body you wanted. When you are doing a L.A.D. exercise you do not become instantly clairvoyant, but in time your capacity for clairvoyant imagery increases. Some of your L.A.D. results will have empathic content, that's fine as long as you understand that when there is no empathic content the L.A.D. is still good.

Chapter 9: Discovering Your Power

A discussion on Gamma can either be made out to be very complex or very simple. The problem with going farther than Delta is that we have run out of brain waves. Delta waves cycle between 1 to 4 per second, so going past Delta seems impossible. In fact, everything about Gamma seems impossible. Yet Gamma experiences occur. Gamma is not related to a specific brain wave pattern, for it is the combination of all brain wave patterns.

Gamma is consciousness as an energy field, a whole unit of interconnected functions. Understanding the "field effect" is a vital turning point in your development. Grasping the implications of the field-effect can take you out of the realm of "superstitious thinking" into a rational and grounded appreciation for empathic functioning. This is an important step in progressing as an empath.

In some older traditions Gamma has been called "the aura," where others have called it the "L-field." It is not limited to your head area or to your psyche. The best image of Gamma is suggested by the Tattwa akasa as a basically oval light surrounding your entire body. (Representing the field effect itself).

Gamma is the source of consciousness combined with the overall effect of consciousness. It is the source of the other levels of empathic communication in Beta, Alpha, Theta, and Delta. As the source of consciousness Gamma could be called the "spirit."

At the Gamma level we enter the world of metaphysical and spiritual speculation, something that is best communicated through Dreamtongue, through symbols, myths, archetypes, ideas, and associations.

Gamma events are the result of the ultimate nature of all things, whatever that may be. Gamma is representative of that "one step beyond our ability to perceive or comprehend." Gamma events are more difficult to explain because they occur outside of our understanding of reality. Gamma events are precognition: empathic messages about future events; retrocognition: empathic messages about past events; communication with other levels of consciousness or beings as they might be called.

At the Gamma level issues of life after death, communication with the deceased, channeling, reincarnation, and the nature of reality all come into play. As I mentioned before, some empaths prefer to work at just the normal empathic levels and do not necessarily go as far as the Gamma level. Gamma is more difficult to work with because it is indefinable, yet at the same time, it is easier to work with because all things are an expression of it.

There is a great paradox at this level; involving the mind trying to know or perceive past its own limits. The results of the paradox, unfortunately, are an endless amount of speculation, fantasy, and wishful thinking. What is "true" or "truth" remains to be seen. That does not mean that we should overlook or avoid the Gamma level. It just means that we should be more vigilant and grounded when it comes to investigating Gamma experience.

At the Gamma level, Dreamtongue occurs in its full expressive form. Communication and information are available through creative and archetypal imagery.

One of the misconceptions that people have about any kind of "psychic functioning" is that it mostly means the ability to tell the future. From this belief, many people who try to develop their empathic natures spend a lot of time focusing on predicting the future in some form. Precognitions do occur but the strength of empathic ability rests in the day to day connections of telepathy, alpha associating, and remote viewing.

The idea that we can predict the future is fraught with many problems. If we can predict the future does that mean, then, that the future is already set? Does learning about future events change future events? If so, then what is the value of learning future events? The idea of seeing into the future presents an unsolvable puzzle to the human mind. It does not fit into any understanding of reality as we know it. Yet it happens.

Information about the future comes from a place inside that cannot be directly manipulated. It is extremely easy for us to fool ourselves. The laws of chance alone make guessing accurate at least half the time. All too often what appears to be an accurate prediction of the future is really the result of guessing, logical, and critical thinking, imagination, and the desire to believe.

Now, having said that, there are awesome moments when images and information about the future actually do come through the empathic mind. Let's just be as realistic about it as we possibly can.

The most common forms of precognition come through dreams. It creates an odd feeling when you walk into a place and meet a person you dreamed about two years before. This feeling has been called deja-vu. It is safe to say that most deja-vu experience comes from empathic dreams that eventually become reality.

Precognition as a empathic ability often occurs spontaneously and without warning. This type of Gamma information suddenly appears in the mind through feelings, impressions, thoughts, or images. Gamma messages can interact with any of the other levels since Gamma is the source place of the levels. The most direct form of precognition is the spontaneous kind, for it usually relates to information that is needed in the moment.

People have tried for centuries, if not millennia, to manipulate precognition. Divination is an art form that has evolved for the purpose of manipulating precognition. The tools of divination help the empath focus their empathic impressions and empathic intent. The common tools of divination include tarot cards, scrying tools, numbers, runes, I-Ching, and yes, even tea leaves.

It does not matter what the tools are for all your empathic mind needs is a place to focus. The use of a visual object to gain empathic information from Gamma is a Beta function. Therefore the use of tools can establish a channel between the Beta and the Gamma levels.

Another form of precognition is the premonition. A premonition is more like a "sense" of something about to occur. People who fly the same airline or airplane all the time are often the ones who decided not to take the flight the day of an accident; because it did not feel right for some reason. A premonition is a Gamma message about a future event that is felt at the Alpha level through a sense or impression.

Gamma interacts with all the empathic levels. Gamma is the power source to the other levels. Working with Gamma strengthens Beta, Alpha, Theta, and Delta functions. To work with Gamma is to develop your power source as an empath and is easy to initiate. To begin working with Gamma only requires that you select a tool or tools that you will use to focus your empathic intent.

Selecting a Gamma Tool

A Gamma tool is one that is used in divination. Divination is the artful way of processing empathic information. Again, traditional tools of divination are the Tarot cards, runes, numbers, tea leaves, crystal balls, a bowl of water, yarrow sticks for I-Ching, regular playing cards, and so on. No one tool is better than the other except that a specific tool will work better for one individual than for another.

Before selecting a tool, be sure to consider the following information. The traditional tools were created by people who were connected to their own Gamma level, their own personal power. The best tools are the ones you develop yourself or the ones that you use in your own personal way. That is why there are so many cards and systems available today.

There is an empathic renaissance occurring. People are realizing the creative force behind empathic and spiritual methodology. If you do choose a traditional tool, then be flexible and realize that it will eventually have to be shaped to fit your own inner nature.

To develop your Gamma power source:

✓ Select one tool. (You may add more later, but the goal is to focus!) The tool may be traditional or one you develop yourself.

✓ The tool needs to be a physical object. If your tool is a "spirit guide" or an empathic totem then create or acquire a physical object that represents your connection to the guide. This can be a piece of jewelry, a picture, a symbolic object, etc.

✓ If the tool is jewelry then take exceptional care of that jewelry. Keep it on your person at all times. When you want to access empathic information touch or gaze at the object. If the tool is a set of cards or other traditional objects then make a special place to keep and preserve them. How you treat the tool forms an "aura" of expectation and preservation of energy.

✓ If you use a box or area to store your Gamma tools, be sure to include an image of your empathic totem on or in the area. We are working with the "art of intent" here, not superstitious thinking. For example, let's say your empathic totem is a hawk and your choice of tools is a set of Tarot cards. You can build or acquire a wooden box to store the cards. You could carve or burn the image of a hawk into the lid of the box. This way you have connected your Gamma tools with your empathic totem. The goal is to have all levels interact.

✓ The use of tools establishes a Beta presence for your empathic nature. You can extend this presence in different ways. Your object or the container of your object can be anointed with a scent that you associate with your empathic nature. The choice of an oil or scent should be made empathically by listening to Dreamtongue: through a Beta, Alpha, Theta, or Delta message. Any colors associated with your tools can be chosen in the same way. The more associations you form to your tools the stronger your connection to your power source.

- ✓ If you find yourself using a tool and you are not feeling connected to it, then change. Do not become burdened with trying to make it work. Your empathic nature is already present; it simply needs a means to express. Listen to your inner empathic, it will guide you.

- ✓ Change and evolve your tools over time. Do not worry about jumping around from one thing to another. You will find yourself always coming back to the thing that empowers you the most. The process of being drawn back to something is a very powerful Gamma confirmation.

Creating Your Own Gamma Tool

The creation of new Gamma tools is very prevalent today. You can find countless versions of Tarot cards, empathic reading cards, and spiritual guidance cards. There are many systems of divination available to you right now. Any one of them may be your Gamma connection. You can also be the creator of one. As an empath you only need a place to focus your attention. Once focused, you can listen to the language of Dreamtongue.

To create your tool or tools first decide what kind of method you want to use. There are two types of method in divination:

- ✓ the "drawing method"-- where empathic information appears to be drawn from a source, and
- ✓ the "projective method" - where empathic information is projected onto images and patterns.

The projective method is commonly done through cards, stones, and patterns. You can design a set of cards which contain images that are meaningful to you. The number of cards, the meaning of the cards, how they are to be laid out, and the guidelines for their use can all be empathically determined by you.

There is no secret formula needed in order for them to work. Your own empathic nature is what works; the tools are just the means to an end. You could grab a clump of dirt and throw it on the sidewalk, then look for patterns in the dirt. It is your empathic mind which organizes the interpretations you get. So, be creative and be adventurous.

The drawing method can be done in many ways. For example, you may select a necklace as your Gamma tool. Let's say it is an ankh. You might rub this ankh with patchouli oil once a week because the scent of patchouli is compatible with your empathic nature. When you smell the patchouli you are reminded of your growth as an empath.

To use the drawing method you would train yourself to touch the ankh in a specific way, such as holding it between the thumb and index finger with your left hand. You associate this act with drawing empathic information into your awareness, so that each time you do this you access one or more levels of Dreamtongue.

Empowering Your Gamma Tools

The last piece to put into place involves connecting with the world around you. As an empath, it is vital that you connect with the Earth, the natural rhythms and cycles that are occurring around you.

- ✓ Select a place outdoors that is special to you in some way. Listen to the Dreamtongue messages you get while selecting an area. Listen to how your body responds, to the feelings you get, the impressions that come to mind, the images that appear. You probably already have such a place in mind; it is a place where you need to go from time to time.
- ✓ It does not matter if this is a public or private place, as much as it matters how you feel and respond to it. It can be a park, a beach, a backyard, a courtyard, a tree, a river, a stream, a pond, a path, a garden. It can be anything as long as it feels right to you and you can associate connecting to the Earth through the place.
- ✓ Make a point to visit this place at least once a week. There are no rules for how often you do this; it is just that you maintain the connection. Sometimes you will need to go there more often and other times less often. There will be times when weather affects your access to the place. The place itself will go through cycles and growth, which will be a part of your

process. If your place is a park that gets bulldozed down for a parking lot then your growth will involve transferring the energy of that spot to a new place.

✓ Take your Gamma tool(s) with you when you go to the place. You may design a ritual (process) for your empowerment time. You may just sit in contemplation. Your time may involve walking or creating or whatever. You must guide and determine these things for yourself. This inner guidance is the power of the empath that you need to develop.

✓ Record each time you visit your power source in your empaths journal. Some may use the time at the power source for journal writing. You may find yourself writing more directly in Dreamtongue (from the empathic level) by doing this.

✓ Always go alone to this place. This maintains the focus and the concentration behind your development. You might desire to share this spot with a special person but its best you keep this practice intact. Of course, the only really guiding principle comes from within you and all choices rest with you. You may find other places that are better for sharing with others.

When you have selected a Gamma tool or tools, and have begun the practice of empowering yourself and those tools, you have mastered your empathic ability.

Chapter 10: Energy Vampires

The problem with being an empath? They show a lot if care. There's nothing wrong with caring in and of itself. In fact, it can be an admirable quality that helps build connection with others in a very unique and intimate way.

The problem, however, is that there are people out there who actively seek out empaths and, if care is not taken, take advantage of how much you care. These people are what's known as energy vampires.

Energy vampires can include family members, friends coworkers or significant others who feed off of the energy of anyone who gives them the time of day. They tend to prey on the sensitive, compassionate types, which is why empaths are perfect targets.

While empaths unfortunately attract energy vampires, that doesn't mean you have to fall victim to their manipulations.

Energy Vampire Traits

Before you can spot an energy vampire, you need to know which traits to look out for to help you identify them. Keep in mind, not all energy vampires will exhibit all of these traits.

Manipulative

The goal with an energy vampire is control, and manipulation is one of the tactics they use to gain it. If you notice someone in your life is always playing with your head to suck you in, then it's important to know that that's not healthy.

Self-centered

You know those people who are always talking about themselves and never ask you anything? If you do, you probably also know it's not just the conversation that revolves around them. It's all other aspects of life as well.

No matter what you do, they don't seem to be concerned with you or your feelings. And that's because they're not.

Plays the Blame Game

It doesn't matter what the situation may be if there's someone to blame, they're ready to point fingers. Energy vampires don't take responsibility for their actions so they're always looking for other people to shift the blame onto.

Melodramatic

When it rains, it doesn't just pour. It's like a torrential storm of doom and gloom. Every problem (big or small) is magnified and made to be worse than it actually is in real life. Or if there is no problem, they have the ability to create one out of nothing — which does take some skill if you think about it.

Think of your typical drama queen and an energy vampires fits the profile perfectly.

Insecure

Everyone has insecurities, but the way energy vampires handle theirs is nothing but negative. When they feel a tinge of insecurity, one way they may handle it is by trying to assert dominance over someone who is weaker than them.

Another way this insecurity may manifest is that they become judgmental to the point where they feel the need to put others down. Because exerting control over another person or putting someone else down gives them a false sense of feeling better about themselves.

Jealous

They're never happy for you. Instead, the things that bring happiness into your life brings jealousy into theirs. So you may notice that they try to undercut your accomplishments or employ some negative tactic in order to bring you back down to their level.

Downers

These people have the ability to always bring the mood down with their negative attitude. You may also know them as a party pooper or wet blanket — different names, but they're one in the same.

Misery loves company, which is why the energy vampires in your life are consciously or unconsciously trying to bring you down to their level.

Traits aren't the only way to identify an energy vampire. It's also important to understand how people in your life make you feel, so pay attention to the following.

- ✓ You can't quite put your finger on why, but something about their presence makes you feel anxious. The relationships you have with energy vampires are unhealthy, and your mental health reflects the chaotic nature of these relationships.
- ✓ The guilt trips just keep coming. As an empath, you're a compassionate and sensitive person, so you want to be there for the people you care about in your life, and energy vampires take advantage of that quality.
- ✓ Energy vampires want to bring you down to their negative level so they can maintain control over you. So if there's someone in your life who's putting you down instead of lifting you up, that's a sign that your relationship with that person is not healthy.

✓ If you constantly feel like you're walking on egg shells with someone in your life, then that's a clue that you may be dealing with an energy vampire. No one is perfect so there are going to be situations where we have to step up and take responsibility for our actions. But that's not the case for the energy vampire.

Because they're always pointing fingers and shifting the blame, you begin to feel like you can't say or do anything right.

How to Protect Yourself

Just because you attract them, doesn't mean you need to fall victim to the tricks of energy vampires. Here are some things you can do to protect yourself.

Recognize the Red Flags Early

Pay attention to the things people do, not what they say. Now that you know the traits to look out for and the ways to spot them, be vigilant about spotting the signs of an energy vampire early on before you get in too deep. So, keep an eye out for red flags that may pop up with people you meet.

As an empath, your caring tendencies can get in the way of your rational mind. You make excuses for people's behavior or try to overlook the faults of others in order to blindly see the good, but all of that does nothing but hurt you in the end.

Set Boundaries

Because you're sensitive and caring, energy vampires can take that as an invitation to walk all over you. Don't allow that to happen.

If you have energy vampires in your life, it's important to set and enforce clear boundaries. That way they know where they stand and the lines they can't cross, which gives you back some of the control in the relationship.

Get on Their Level

Empaths have the tendency to give without ever expecting anyone to give in return. In most cases, there's nothing wrong with this tendency because most people choose to give back and create a reciprocal relationship.

However, as you probably already know at this point, energy vampires don't reciprocate, they take. So the relationship between an empath and energy vampire becomes imbalanced and negatively impacts the empath in the situation.

So, pay attention to how much you're giving to others. And if you notice that someone in your life doesn't reciprocate your generosity, it's in your best interest to scale things back.

Learn to Say "No"

Saying "no" is hard for most people. But as an empath, it can be that much more difficult. This goes back to setting boundaries. Turning people down and rejecting things that aren't in your best interest is a powerful feeling. So, practice and say "no" when it's appropriate.

Cut Them out Completely

If all else fails, the best course of action may be to cut the energy vampires out of your life completely. It may seem harsh, but energy vampires aren't looking out for your best interest so you need to look out for yourself.

This isn't always possible for some people, but if you can do it, you'll notice that a huge weight has been lifted off of your shoulders.

Chapter 11: The Empath Training Toolkit

While it's easy to blame sensitivity as the cause of our suffering, in reality, our sensitivity isn't to blame. Instead, it is our approach to sensitivity, and therefore to other people, that is responsible for our pain.

Without sensitivity, life loses its magic. Those of that were taught by our parents or societies to perceive sensitivity as a weakness never revealed the full picture. In reality, it is sensitivity that allows us to experience a life of depth. It is sensitivity that allows us to listen to our deepest needs and dreams. It is sensitivity that allows us to be of service to others. It is sensitivity that permits us to perceive the intricate beauty and divinity of life.

Sensitivity is a powerful and vital element of life. Without it, we can't soulfully mature into the people we are destined to become. In fact, it is sensitivity that allows us to experience spiritual awakenings. And it is sensitivity that allows us to discover the deepest kind of truth, joy and peace.

Reprogramming the way you perceive your sensitivity is the first tool in your toolkit. Without changing your perceptions of sensitivity, you will unconsciously sabotage any progress you wish to make. So ensure that you explore your feelings about the concept of sensitivity!

The best way to do this is by writing down the word "sensitivity" and immediately recording any words that come to mind.

Then, you can think about times in your life when your sensitivity actually helped you. For example, words such as "pain," "acute," and "sharp" might come to mind when you try this activity. These words reveal a lot about your perception towards sensitivity; namely that it is

something "negative." After you have recorded the immediate words that pop into your mind, you can examine how your sensitivity has actually helped you in the past. For example, you might discover that your sensitivity has helped you to save your partner from being fired, your child do better in school or helped you to make wise decisions about your life. I recommend that you write down as many situations as you can think of. This will help you to slowly reprogram your thinking patterns about sensitivity.

Set Rules and Boundaries

The reason why you likely feel anxious and depressed is because you haven't set rules and boundaries for yourself in the past. This is normal and natural: most empaths, healers and highly sensitive people neglect to do this when young because they haven't had any role models or any guidance.

You don't need to be a disciplinarian or a nun to set rules and boundaries for yourself; you just need a healthy understanding of the difference between "comfortable" and "uncomfortable. " Take some time out to sit by yourself in a quiet place and reflect on what places, people and situations make you feel comfortable, as opposed to uncomfortable. For example, you might discover that you feel very unsettled around a particular person at work because they suck the beauty out of life. Perhaps this person is negative, bitter, and judgmental. Or perhaps you might discover that you feel calm and balanced in a certain area of your house, or place outside. You might even discover that the source of your anxiety or depression is triggered by the environment you live in, the temperature, the lack of nature, the weather, the pollution, and so forth.

Setting boundaries is about limiting your exposure to uncomfortable situations, places, or people. You can master these situations later, but first, you need a real break from them, finding solace in what makes you feel balanced, comfortable, and calm.

Learn to Actively Go Into Your Pain

It sounds counter-intuitive doesn't it, "going into your pain"! But it's a very important step to releasing the pent up energy inside of you. When we are preoccupied by escaping, repressing and avoiding our pain, we perpetuate the cycle of our suffering. Rather than giving in to the temptation to run – stop – be still.

Sit down and let yourself feel the fatigue, the confusion, the anger, the hurt. Only once you face the truth of the pain you feel can you then progress to the next stage of letting the suffering go.

Learn to Distinguish Your Emotions

Yes, you might soak up the emotions of others like a sponge, but that doesn't mean that you are exempt from creating and deeply experiencing, your own emotions. It is all too easy to portray ourselves as victims in life, and much harder to take responsibility for our own happiness. A key realization on the path of healing as an empath is to learn to distinguish what you are feeling from what others are feeling. And there isn't always a clean cut distinction. Often you will find that you are feeling about 45% of the emotions, and others are feeling about 55% of the emotions, or you might be feeling 20% and others 80%, and vice versa.

Develop Healthy Self-Esteem

Empaths with low self-esteem will suffer much more than those with healthy and balanced self-esteems. Obvious? Perhaps. But not always. Being an empath can be confusing, and it can be very easy to blame the hopelessness and worthlessness we feel on the bombardment of stimuli we experience every day. It helps to realize that the more love, respect and trust you develop in yourself, the less you suffer, and that thoughts such as "I'm cursed, " "I'm so weird and different from everybody, " "I hate being an empath" and so forth, are all often products of low self-esteem.

Catharsis is Vital

As an empath, it is so important that you incorporate some consistent form of catharsis into your everyday routine to rid yourself of the stuffy energy you might be harboring.

Favored forms of catharsis among empaths include journaling/writing, meditation, walking and jogging. Other forms of catharsis include singing, dancing, screaming (privately), laughing and crying. It is also extremely beneficial as an empath to teach yourself how to get in touch with your body – I call this "bodymindfulness" or "somatic mindfulness. " Basically, learning to be in touch with your body is an excellent way of anchoring and grounding yourself in the present moment rather than getting lost in the flood of emotions and sensations that come your way. Bodymindfulness is also a good way of learning to listen to your needs, as well as nurturing and taking care of yourself.

Know When to Draw an Emotional Line

As a sensitive person, it can be hard to accept that the pain of other people is theirs to bear, not yours. You have your own cross to bear. This can be hard to realize, especially when you have the tendency to internalize the pain of others.

Remember that there is only so much you can genuinely do to help other people. Of course, you can try to help them or guide them as much as you see fit, but at the end of the day the person experiencing the original pain must be willing to help themselves for any true healing to occur. Often, your caring nature blind you to the fact that many people don't want, or aren't prepared to be fixed because they are content in the safety of their misery.

Be Gentle With Yourself

When we lose touch with our sensitivity, it is common for us to start mistreating and abusing ourselves without knowing it. Subtle forms of self-abuse include binge eating, eating toxic food, not sleeping enough, not getting enough sunlight, staying indoors too much, pressuring ourselves to be perfect, unconsciously acting out our core beliefs, and many other forms of self-sabotage.

Being gentle with yourself is an art because it requires practice. As a highly sensitive or empathic person, it is vital that you realize that in order to be compassionate with others you must first learn how to be compassionate with yourself.

Reclaim Your Inner Strength

Deep down inside, beyond the veil of your superficial appearance, you harbor something quiet, but powerful. Your gifts don't dominate, tyrannize or overthrow people, but that doesn't detract from their strength, or usefulness. If anything, your powerful but subtle gifts benefit you more in the long term, allowing you to gather emotional, psychological and physical information from your surroundings that is often inaccessible and undisclosed to the average, unreceptive mind. This is the advantage you have as a sensitive and intuitive person.

Being an empath can be difficult and confusing, but with awareness of your gifts and abilities, you can refine them and use them to guide, heal and protect yourself and the people you love.

Chapter 12: Harnessing Your Abilities

So you have all these abilities, but you are blocked from using them as long as you are not in control of your sensitivities. So how do you learn control? There are three parts to understanding and harnessing your empathic abilities.

Untrained empathic ability always leads to emotional confusion and burnout. To begin to control your abilities is to know where these problems are coming from: what they feel like, where you are weakest, how you can become stronger and more competent in navigating and understanding your own mental landscape.

Even if you succeed, holding yourself to this standard of self honesty takes constant work, maintenance, and a special blend of forgiveness and determination. You will be forced to confront your biases, your weaknesses, your most basic needs and where they come from. But in the end, knowing that personal landscape, ups and downs, easy and rough patches, will lend you an incredible resilience, strength, and a solid foundation for your abilities.

Know Thyself

There is an ancient proverb: in Greek it is gnothi seauton, in Latin, temet nosce. In English, it is usually phrased "Know Thyself". The goal must be to take control of our mind and emotions by understanding them.

Emotions doesn't come out of nowhere for anyone. We become angry or sad or happy not because there is some set response to each moment, or because people "make" us feel a certain way. Our emotions are clues to our internal landscape. This landscape is shaped by all our experiences, and in turn shapes our ideas, emotions, and tendencies.

If someone says something to make you angry, your first reaction cannot be just to squash down the anger, and certainly isn't just reacting with knee-jerk rage; I need to ask a question: Why? Why am I angry? What about this person, this statement, this moment is making me see red? Is it actually that I am hurt by their opinion of me? Why do I care about that opinion? Is it that I find their statement offensive? Why am I offended? It is when you can take a moment and find honest but non-judgemental answers to those questions that you can begin not only to act instead of merely react, but begin to shape and understand your own emotional landscape.

This ability to see and sculpt our biases, tendencies, and problems internally is a human trait; we have both the ability to reason and reflect and the power to choose our actions. As empaths who can pick up the emotions and biases of others from moment to moment, we must be extra vigilant. To act peacefully, serenely, and objectively we must first understand ourselves deeply, to see what makes each of us tick. This process requires frequent, frank self-examination, and meditation is the most effective way to do that. If you are new to meditation I suggest you experiment with these two meditations before you begin the following one.

The Calming Breath

Carve out a little time where you will not be disturbed, where you can be by yourself and think. Sometimes it helps to write, or speak aloud what your thoughts are, or you can keep them in your mind. Also keep in mind that as you do this it will become a faster and more natural process, and you can start to practice it before, during, and after moments of stress or high emotion to help you act instead of react.

Close your eyes, and breathe naturally and deeply. Let the darkness behind your eyelids and the coolness of the air in your lungs calm your mind.

What are you feeling, right now at this moment? What ideas or emotions begin to float to the surface of your consciousness? Try to tease apart the ball of tangled feelings that is normal for most people. Don't let this stress you out: all you are here to do is look at who you are, not who you were, or could be. You are not here to judge or regret. Examine your emotions as you would the horizon, or a familiar but new object in your hands. What is there? Likely there will be one or two things that pull your attention in particular. Let yourself be pulled, examining those closely. How do you know that you feel this way? Are there physical sensations, like tightness in your throat, chest, or shoulders, associated with those feelings? Are there memories or events that come up when you examine these feelings? Remember to keep breathing and relax as you continue.

Next, delve a little deeper. Why are you feeling these emotions now? What sparked them? It could be something specific, or as nebulous as a rough week. Think about what parts of yourself could spawn these emotions. Are you nervous about your position at work? Worried about a friend? Conflicted about who you are, or what you want? No judgment is attached to whatever you reveal, you are merely following a stream back to its source.

Lastly, what is this emotional reaction based on? We feel emotion, especially strong emotion, as a response to fundamental needs that are either being filled or not, such as our need for love, stability, approval, and independence. When we lack a fundamental need, or feel it is threatened somehow (assessments not always based on logic or reality), we are often swamped with emotions like fear, insecurity, and anger. Has someone changed or challenged a firmly held or fundamental belief? Are you feeling trapped, or insecure in your life somewhere? If you find that your emotion comes from a lack or need, how can you fill and stabilize that need? Is it healthy for you to do so? If not, how can you learn to be less dependent on that need? Give yourself space to feel the emotion and recognize it, and make a note of all you've learned. As you do this more, you will start to understand yourself and your reactions in a new way, and start to be able to predict and control how you react or will react based on past experience or recognition of small signals and clues your mind and body give you. All this meditation is about is selfunderstanding, gaining knowledge that will help you shape yourself and your actions in the future, so anything you learn is important on your path to emotional wellness and unbiased understanding.

This meditation is not a one-and-done activity. You will have to incorporate this kind of productive, non-judgmental self-reflection into your meditative routine, and learn to do it on the fly. This way, when you feel an emotion out of nowhere, you will soon be able to identify if it's something rooted in your psyche, or if it truly belongs to someone else. This is step one on the process of separating your emotional headspace from those around you.

Building a Foundation

Now that you are starting to understand your own emotional landscape, it's time to shore up yourself and your progress. There are several ways to do this, and we will focus on those that help shore up the areas where empaths tend to wear out quickly or be weakest in.

As an empath, you give too much space to others' emotional lives. You solve their problems with ease and help them restore equilibrium, often at the expense of your own energy stores. In order to avoid depleting your ability to give back to others need well-defined boundaries.

Some of us may never have had or witnessed what strong, healthy boundaries look like, so lets delve into that a bit. Think of boundaries as rules set up to protect you in sensible ways. They change as you do, and sometimes apply to different people differently. They are the lines you set that say what you will and won't allow.

Learn to take time and space for yourself, communicate your needs carefully and without guilt about the space and energy you are taking up, and make sure that as you use or dole out your physical, social, spiritual, emotional and mental energies, you are choosing intentionally and actively to do so, not reacting to the needs of others. Not only is this more satisfying, but it will help tremendously with feelings of being overdrawn or extended.

Creating boundaries isn't just a matter of mental discipline or making choices about other people. You do need to know where other people begin (in terms of their responsibility, interactions and expectations with and for you, or their energetic and emotional presence), but you also need to know where you end. The 'Know Yourself' exercise is an excellent way to bring your awareness into your emotional space and attend to, deal with, and validate your emotional needs. However emotions have physical ramifications as well, and empaths often find that emotions can get stuck somewhere inside you, even if they aren't your own. You need to bring awareness into your body.

Imagine that you've left to visit a friend in another city and forgotten to lock your house. And that's not all: You've left all the doors and windows wide open, so anyone can get in.

This is what it's like to be an empath. You can abandon your own home, your direct experience, in favor of someone else's. The more you do this [without locking up], the more difficult it is to return. What makes matters worse is that not inhabiting your body (and the moment) keeps the benefits of mindfulness-based practices just beyond your reach."

It is an amazing advantage to be able to experience someone else's direct experience, but to do so without training and control is to abandon your sense of self, your own boundaries, a bit at a time. That being said, bringing awareness into your body, through exercise, meditation, physical contact and affection, and self-care (baths, walks in the park, reading a good book etc.) can help you learn what it feels like to live in just your body, and feel just your thoughts.

Be present, get to know who you are, and feel rooted in yourself and confident in your space. That way you know what it should feel like as you start to build healthy boundaries with those around you. This also includes taking a break from spaces that add to your emotional 'noise' (and yes that includes social media or the internet).

Become Space

To begin, take a few deep breaths to relax. Close your eyes and focus on the space inside yourself, between the molecules of your body. Expand that space, out in every direction. Expand all of the cells in your body, even the space within the individual atoms of your body. Expand that space, and your entire body with it, and fill the room you are in. Then continue expanding, to fill the building. Then, your town. Then your state/region. Continue expanding to your country, and then the whole earth. Keep expanding, until you are present throughout the solar system, and onward to the galaxy until you fill the entire universe! Don't latch onto anything or look, just expand and breathe. Stay here as long as you'd like, just sensing what is there but not holding onto anything.

As you expand, you will notice there is a sensation of matter stuck between the spaces (they may be physical, such as tension in your lungs or between your eyebrows, or mental/emotional such as holding your breath, feeling stressed or heavy, feeling distracted). Breath into those areas of tightness or density, and let anything stuck in the net of your being float away or dissolve. As you slowly come back together remain aware of yourself, emotionally and physically. Sometimes a last sort of energetic shake is required (or just feels nice), like a dog shaking off water. Take one last deep deep breath, and exhale slowly but intentionally, pushing any sort of emotional or energetic detritus you might feel on the outside of your skin or aura off into the air, into nothingness, the same way you might blow dust off of a table.

Many people who struggle with their empathic ability often just want to turn it off or make it stop. Empaths, especially those that have made it to adulthood without any training or without developing some kind of coping mechanism, but with their abilities intact are frequently exhausted, overwhelmed, and despairing. I say intact, because it is possible to lose your empathic abilities.

Not knowing how to deal with the sensory input, feeling overwhelmed and exhausted, and receiving judgment from their peers for being 'too sensitive' or 'unable to take a joke' or being told that they are acting immature, some people purposefully stamp out or cut themselves off from that part of themselves, often permanently damaging their ability to interact emotionally with the people around them, even those they are closest to. This thinking should be discouraged. Empathic ability can be exhausting and stressful, but the ability is not the problem. Distress and pain is a sign of a problem that needs fixing; if you stop feeling the pain, it doesn't solve the problem; it merely buries it, allowing the issue to become worse, more complex, and more difficult to solve or heal.

Many empaths with interest in energy work resort to constantly cleansing their aura, treating the symptoms instead of the cause; this might make you feel better, but it can't be all that you do. Meditations like 'become space' should be used whenever they are necessary, and are part of regular maintenance, but a real solution does not just treat the symptoms.

Another common solution is shielding, or blocking out all of this extra emotional input. I do not encourage this as a regularly used or permanent strategy because it can create unhealthy emotional distance, and make the affected empath seem cold, aloof, and socially inept (as most of them do not realize how much they rely on their abilities in everyday situations); it can also be frankly exhausting and unhealthy to cut off or block off a natural part of yourself. You also block yourself from using your abilities, which is a shame (can't sense others emotions if they can't get in ever). However in an emergency (to prevent panic attack, to deal with a traumatic event in the short term, or if you just need a quick fix to stop feeling so overwhelmed), you can temporarily shield yourself from the emotions of others. Use these techniques like you would an umbrella in a rainstorm: you'd be silly to not use one to keep you dry if you have it, but its not something you can live under permanently to avoid ever getting wet. This is also a great exercise for our future, more stable, techniques, especially if you are new to energy work.

If energy is not your thing or part of your beliefs, that is perfectly fine. Treat these exercises as a visualization meditation, envisioning the imagery as a way to root you back into the present moment or distract you from whatever overwhelming sensation that might prompt you to explore these exercises.

Shielding

Shielding feels different for everyone, just as energy feels different for everyone, but the technique is the same. Feel for the energy around you, your personal aura or force, or just bring your awareness into the present moment. Find a metaphor that makes you feel protected and insulated from harm: perhaps it's a memory of hiding under the sheets as a kid, warm and soft and invisible, or perhaps its something more fantastical, like clear diamond-hard walls being thrown up around you; whatever imagery feels strongest or most appealing to you in that moment is what will work best. Use your empathic strength to embody that feeling, really imagine and feel what that would feel like. As you do so, pull your own energy around you, solidifying it into your vision to hold it in place. Pull any sensory information into making this vision stronger; the sensation of wrapping a blanket around yourself, perhaps the sound of rain on an umbrella, or scent of a moment in time where you felt safe. Stay in your protective bubble as long as you need to, meditating, or focusing long enough to get through what needs to be done during your crisis. Shields take focus to maintain (even when you store them in an object or after much practice), so be careful to stay grounded and not overextend the energy you have by keeping them up longer than necessary, and take care of yourself afterwards, both because of whatever you needed shielding from and because of the aftereffects of energy work/extended focus and meditation (which are most easily counteracted by physical contact, warm water, such as showering, washing your hands, drinking tea, and eating; essentially, taking care of your physical body will bring you more fully back into your physical body).

Growing Strong Roots and Grounding Yourself

Grounding is a key part of being a successful and balanced empath. Rooting yourself into your space and into reality is an excellent way not only to build the kind of strength and awareness these self-reflective practices require, but to learn to meet your own needs and build healthy boundaries and healthy bonds between you and those around you. Grounding is, at it's most basic, a way to grow roots. Empaths often dissociate mentally and emotionally as a way to 'get away' from all the noise, and as a result we become flighty and unstable. Just as we dissociate in all these ways, so we need to ground in all of those ways. Physically the best way to do this is through touch and exercise. Self-care, cuddling, platonic or nonplatonic hugs, wearing your coziest sweater, laying in the grass, taking a bath, all of these things can bring you back down to earth and root you into your physical form, as well as strengthen the appreciation and bond you have for your physical self. Humans are tactile beings, so lean into touch in ways that make you happy. Exercise, especially core exercises such as low back and abdomen exercises, as well as practices like restorative yoga (which relies on gravity, the original grounding force, to stretch and strengthen your body) also help combat physical ungroundedness, and strengthen the energy centers that empaths often weaken through uncontrolled emotion hopping. Mentally we can ground ourselves by listening attentively to others and ourselves with an eye to our own growth. Things like journaling, active listening, and reading or watching media that helps us understand and grow in our ideas and opinions, can help ground you mentally. Especially writing or talking about why you believe what you believe, or think what you think, can be a great grounding activity. The more you understand and are open and confident about your intellect and beliefs, the more grounded and relaxed you feel mentally. Particularly useful are the emotional and spiritual/energetic methods of grounding. These can include spending time in nature, exploring and discussing your feelings with a non-judgmental partner, therapist, or journal, and meditations involving emotional digging (such as the Know Yourself meditation at the beginning) or forgiving yourself. The most commonly practiced method of grounding is a simple energetic exercise that people do before and after practicing energy work.

Basically it involves releasing your extra energies and tensions into the ground or universe, but remaining open to the universal force, so that the flow and exchange of energy within you is smooth, connected, and stable. You should feel rooted and solid, just like the tree used in the first exercise in the link. Again, all of these can be done as either visualization meditations, or energy work depending on your preferences and understanding of the Force. Here is another more involved grounding exercise I developed. Before I begin this meditation, I want to stress that your anchor cannot be another person, as it is the empath's tendency to meld with those the feel close or reliable around them, which exacerbates the relationship and the empath's own stability and boundaries.

Finding an Anchor

We all need to ground ourselves from time to time. This is a great meditation to do at the end of the day, or when feeling overwhelmed. It is also a particularly useful meditation for empaths, or people who are feeling panicked, dissociated, disphoric, ungrounded, or unsafe about something in their life. Get comfortable. Light some candles, dim the lights, and find a nice pillow to sit on. If you have a little fountain or some soft indistinct background music (basically some soothing white noise), that can also be helpful.

If the room is chilly, maybe drape a robe or a blanket around your shoulders. Sit comfortably, either in a chair or on the floor with your spine upright in its natural curves, as if a string attached to the crown of your head was pulling you upwards. Close your eyes. Take a nice deep, slow breath, in through your nose, and release it slowly with your mouth closed. Continue breathing at your own pace with slow, deep breaths. Let everything but the sound of your breath, the light smoky scent of the candles and the awareness of this quiet space around you drop away. When you feel ready, begin to catalog your thoughts and feelings from the day. Don't try to relive or re-feel them; pick them up and examine them as if they were personal and interesting objects on a table in front of you.

Assess what feelings have broken through, overwhelmed you, or have been making ripples in your usual demeanor. What is the origin of that feeling, where is it coming from? Don't push for answers; let them float up as you calmly probe the experience. When you have an answer, let the feeling sink back down, or quietly tuck it away into the corner of your mind, like putting something back onto its designated space on a neat, quiet shelf. Do this as many times as you need to. When no more difficulties or thoughts seem to present themselves, focus yourself on your chosen anchor. An anchor is something that makes you feel rooted and safe, something you have deep but uncomplicated feelings for. You may choose anything you wish, an idea, a principle, a memory, but in my opinion, the ideal anchor is the earth itself. Earth is solid, it is our home; it nourishes us, and literally anchors us to its surface with gravity as it whirls through space. It is heavy, solid, and reliable, with enough spiritual weight as an idea on its own to require very little work for it to serve as an anchor.

Whatever you choose, let it be a stable form, an anchor for your consciousness. Picture earth, our beautiful blue and green globe, floating in your mind. Feel the weight of it anchoring you down, both physically with its gravity, and emotionally. Feel rooted like a tree digging its roots through the soil, and protected like the warm weight of heavy blankets on a cold day. Like silt settling to the bottom of a deep dark lake, let the solidity and safety of your anchor help the tumult of the day and anything that has been bothering you sink down from the surface of your awareness and dissolve. You are like a buoy on the surface of that lake, floating calmly on its surface, but firmly tethered to the earth. Continue breathing deeply.

Let that solidity and weight make you more aware of your body; notice any soreness in your muscles, or tension in your face. Slowly scan across your body, breathing into and releasing any tension you find, starting at the top of your head and ending with your legs and feet. Sit with the warm weight and safety of feeling grounded and solid for as long as you like. When you are finished, take a long deep breath and start to breathe regularly again. Open your eyes slowly, stretch carefully, and unfold. ~*~ Knowing yourself well, building a strong emotional foundation, and learning to stay more grounded are not one and done kinds of strategies. All of the methods in this course require maintenance, just as you need to shower most days, or get your hair cut to keep it healthy. All three of these elements combine to create a mindfulness practice that should protect you from the worst of the emotional storms empaths face, while helping you to develop a better sense of self and emotional strength. They require weekly if not daily practice; find ways of breathing and meditating related to them that you could do on the fly; quick check-ins at work or a scan of your feelings in the shower. Incorporate them into your life and pay close attention to the ways in which you start to see the world un-fog. Perhaps you see that someone that was stressful in your life is no longer someone healthy to be around, or ways in which you have been holding yourself back from success or intimacy.

So we have the tools to build emotional control and awareness, and separate your emotions from the emotions of others.

Chapter 13: Using Your Abilities

Before we dive into the specifics of how to train and use your empathic abilities, there are a couple things to discuss; building in long-term protections and strategies, and discussing the particular dark sides of empathic ability.

Empathic Shadow Side: The Manipulator

Empaths can have access to an incredible wealth of very personal, private information, are skilled at reading others, and often know just the right thing to say. People trust you and share themselves with you, both accidentally and happily. These are all powers that can be used for good and healing, but they are a tremendous responsibility. Just as if you could read someone's thoughts, or had been told an important secret, you do, in some way, have power over those around you, frequently without them knowing it, and this can be a tremendous temptation, a pull towards the dark side.

We all have shadow sides. Every skill has a way to misuse it, and every moment is a choice between doing the right thing or not.

Every empath has or will make mistakes along their path, some bigger than others, but an empath perseveres, fixes their mistakes, and makes the right choice the next time. It is no different with your ability. Seeing the places where you could manipulate someone doesn't make you a bad person. Even being tempted to do so (and you will be sometimes) doesn't make you a bad empath. But acting on those dark-side impulses, giving in to the perfectly healthy emotions of anger, envy, fear, etc. and using your talent for personal gain or to harm others is not empath behavior.

Sensing Other's Emotions Safely

So we've spent all this time increasing your own self awareness, building emotional knowledge and stability, and shedding any emotional weight you no longer need or that didn't belong to you in the first place, and we have methods for avoiding it in the future, and solving the problem when we mess up.

You already know how to sense the emotions of others; you've likely been doing it instinctively or accidentally, or had them shoved at you when it comes to particularly intense emotions. Now we can learn to do it purposefully. Pay attention to what it feels like when you do this; that way you can recognize what is happening to you if you start to do so accidentally or randomly, and pull back or control the experience. Also notice what feelings of your own emerge as you allow yourself to feel and understand the feelings of others.

During a conversation with someone, (nothing heavy or stressful) breathe naturally and bring your attention to your own self: remember how you feel and what the amalgamation of emotion and sensory experience that makes up your sense of self feels like, then extend your awareness outward gently towards the other person. Can you tell what is yours or what is not? What are you feeling, and what do you feel from them? Do you have a sense of how they feel or the way in which they function internally? How does this information alter or enhance the information you are already receiving from their body language, word choice, and your knowledge of this person? Practice this regularly, not letting anything you sense stick on, but stretch out beyond yourself, then retreating back into your own space. It's usually a good idea to let someone know you might be practicing this, so they don't get confused or weirded out if the first several times you get a little spacey or distracted. Another method is to open yourself up. Take a deep breath and stretch your energy so you feel open, receptive, as if there is new space inside or immediately around you, and see what comes. Do you feel anything, either physical sensations, or emotions? Where are they coming from? Can you identify what is going on? And then on your next exhale expand back into that space, gently pushing the emotions or sensations back from you where they came from. The goal here is to interact with emotions without melding or drowning in them.

Your regular exercises have strengthened your awareness of who you are and what feelings and energies are yours; use your awareness of that as a way to stay separate, but feel and understand the information that comes your way. Sometimes you'll get hit by a big wave of emotion, whether it's something lovely like joy or excitement, or something intense like anger, fear, or vitriol. These waves can swamp even the most dedicated empath, especially if they are coming from someone who is very close to you. We all have a tendency to wear away the boundaries between us and our loved ones, as a method of getting closer to them. This is not necessarily unhealthy. Although we all need sensible and healthy boundaries with our loved ones, where you place those and what kinds are good for you is up to you as an individual. To cut off or alter those boundaries merely because they can also occasionally be weaknesses is counterproductive. To avoid losing our cool and being swamped by the strong emotions of people close to us, I often use visualization.

Building a Filter

We are looking for a way to share and sense a feeling without it settling on our own being when the emotional pressure gets intense, so the best image for this is a filter. Imagine a fine mesh over wherever you feel the emotion hitting you, physically or emotionally; it might be over your face, or heart, or even a different one of your chakras; no need to expend the focus to surround your body like you would a shield, as the goal is merely to catch some of the extra energy coming at you before it has a chance to impact. There's still energy exchange through the mesh, but the filter catches emotional debris as it streams towards you, the kind of thing that would upset, hurt, or unbalance you, or rob you of your ability to act in that situation.

Let the debris slide off the filter easily, or burn up as it touches it. Obviously, holding an image while you listen or interact naturally with someone going through an intense emotion requires a good deal of focus, but with practice, it becomes something you can switch on in your mind when you require, just like we can close the screen door when mosquitos come out at night.

Practicing Sending and Receiving Emotion

This exercise works best with other empaths, as you can take turns going back and forth, but you can easily practice with non-empaths as well. People with experience in energy work that aren't empaths might also be able to sense the emotions when they are sent with purpose. Sit across from your partner and have them pick a fairly simple emotion (an uncomplicated joyful memory, thinking of a lost pet they still miss, a phobia they might have, etc). If the person wants to or is capable, have them intentionally project that emotion in your direction, and, reaching out with your feelings, see if you can pick it up.

Sometimes sensing straightforward emotion like this will have physical sensations, colors, or even specific ideas attached to them, depending on the sensitivity of the participants, or if either of them have things like synesthesia. Try not to guess and take your time. Interpret whatever you are receiving; is there an emotion you associate with a tightness in your chest or throat? What does the color purple make you feel? Then state what you think you are receiving, and discuss with your partner. Try and take a few deep breaths and shake off the previous round between each turn, and switch back and forth so both people get to try both roles. Through discussion you should be able to figure out a bit where the miscommunication or any difficulties are, and slowly get more accurate as you and your partner get more comfortable.

The energetic/visualization side is not enough to improve your ability; the other half is to understand humanity and the people you interact with better, to be able to follow and project their logic and feelings. Here are other resources to pursue this goal.

- ✓ Active Listening: Don't try and jump ahead, even if you already know what people are going to say. How they say it and when they say it matters, and it builds trust and respect between the person talking and the listener.

- ✓ Expand your social circle: Socialize or interact with more than just people you already know. If you can find people to hang out with that are quite different from you in situation and experience, even better. This is especially true for people who have had very different experiences of society than yourself. Broaden your emotional horizons.

- ✓ Practice Emotions: This sounds silly, but practice feelings that you don't get to feel regularly. Play pretend. Pretend to be Captain America and feel a paladin-y sense of Justice and Righteousness. With a little more care (especially for those of you with conditions like PTSD or sensitive triggers), imagine what it would be like to be panicked by shots whizzing by, or fighting off someone much stronger than yourself, or holding someone you love as they die, or lovely things like finding a first love or having a child or changing the world. Emotions are healthy and natural, and the more you can imagine, the more likely you can recognize and act on the information you will receive as an empathy. Play pretend, cry at movies, get obsessed with books and stories.

✓ Practice self-care: Take care of your physical, social, emotional, spiritual, and mental needs. Working towards wellness in all these areas is a must for all Jedi, but the happier and more stable you feel as a baseline, the easier it is to use and control your abilities healthily and easily.

✓ Talk to those you care about: Let people around you know when you're having a rough time; your ability to let the emotions of others slide off you will be lower, just like we can do less when we catch a cold. You are responsible for your actions, and empathic ability is never an excuse for bad behavior on your part, but letting people you know and love about your abilities or at least that you are feeling sensitive and to be a little gentle with you goes a long way towards building yourself back up.

Chapter 14: How to Strengthen Your Empathic Abilities

Once you learn how not to absorb other people energy, the next step is to devote to expand your intuitive faculties and train yourself to increase the focus of your attention.

Every psychic empath has a unique way of dealing with things. An efficient approach to train yourself to sustain your psychic vision for long periods is to create a mental image in your mind's eye and test to see for how much time you can poise it in your mind.

Although it may seem like a task for newbies, holding a sensory focus from several moments to several minutes before being distraught by the mind requires fantastic efforts.

The human mind is quite changeable and loves to hop from one topic to another without letting you choose if you want to think it. The ego of man is constantly looking for a way to be in a position of power or to pump up its pride or to be in control of the situation. Our goal has always been to separate from that part of us.

In order to develop your empathic psychic abilities, sustain a mental picture of an object for a minimum 15 seconds. You can adjust the seconds to your own choice based on your current level of focus and work your way up through mindful breathing every day.

Try to not only increase the seconds you exert into maintaining an image in your mind but to picture in as much clarity and aliveness as possible. As it is said countless time with many things, it is not about the quantity, it is about the quality.

But do not worry, as you put your efforts in making the mental picture as clear and as vivid as possible you will adjust unaware to doing it for larger periods.

Within your first week of doing it, visualize a simple colored dot or a spiral, with a color of your choice, be it a color you are drawn to advance considerably. When you start to making encouraging progress, you can make the practice more fun and beneficial in the meantime by decorating the picture with extra details.

To improve your empathic abilities, it is important that you go for a simpler object in the beginning to a more detailed one. After a week or two of constant practice, you will be amazed at how good you have become in keeping visual focus when tuning into things. Because by the time you notice it, you will have a clear, vivid psychic vision from your higher self or spirit guides that you connect to. The blurry or vague pictures will be replaced with colorful and lively pictures.

When you teach yourself to hold your vision for longer periods of time, the ability to extract more information will improve too. It's all about working internally with consistency.

Another brilliant way to hone your empathic abilities is to concentrate on keeping an emotion in your heart. This way you nurture your intuitive side and you keep a positive emotion within your heart.

A positive emotion could be the wonderful feeling of deep affection or of fondness that is capable of absorbing the whole heart, mind & body. The emotion can feel like a breathing organism and it can feel loving and as lightness.

Pursue to charge yourself with this feeling and spread it around every corner of your body. You want to be able to hold it there for as much time as possible and to silence your mind to allow your kind and powerful intuition to present itself.

This type of exercise is perfect for empaths who wish to deepen their intuition faculties through visualization or through experiencing emotions.

Every second that you spend in flourishing a positive emotion in your heart space counts. It does not improve your capacity to decipher more complex information coming through the spiritual medium but to feed your soul with it for longer periods of time.

Why this empathic ability serves you well is because when you encounter a negative person like an energy vampire or a narcissist that perceive you as a pray to their energy cravings, you will experience no problems connecting with your heart, your intuitive side and to effortlessly recreate the emotion you have practiced, thus creating an invisible barrier through which the presence of energy vampires and narcissists cannot penetrate.

The power to immediately tap into a safe and loving environment within you at your command is priceless. That is exactly what holding emotional focus offers to you.

And as everything else, you can refine your skill by amplifying or implementing further minor details to your mental object or by increasing the beauty of the emotions that you are feeling.

Amazingly, you can introduce a variety of emotions into your heart space. You can welcome kindness, you can welcome appreciation, you can welcome affection and arrange these emotions one over another like several coats of emotions and see how much can you hold at the same time.

Last but not least, you can inform yourself about the endocrine gland and its state by the time you hit puberty, where an awful and somewhat unknown process of crystallization occurs, leading to losing your psychic power ultimately. Here is a post that can help you counter the effects of crystallization.

Chapter 15: The Reward of Developing Your Empathic Abilities.

Sustaining several emotions in your heart space or mental objects at the same time gives birth to your own multi-dimensional consciousness.

Traditionally, our brain is accustomed to interpreting things in a linear way. However, developing a multi-dimensional consciousness, on the other hand, makes it possible to work with multiple things at the same time.

A multi-dimensional consciousness refines the ability to maintain one feeling in your physical space to several independent from each other feelings, to hold several ideas inhabiting your mind.

And that is what learning how to sustain your psychic focus teaches you – multidimensionality. That is the way to advance your clairvoyance abilities.

The fascinating thing about this exercise is that it is not only valid for clairvoyance but it is also applicable to other innate spiritual gifts.

Clairaudience is one of the many empathic abilities that can be enhanced by drawing your attention to sounds and voices from your immediate surroundings. The Solfeggio frequencies are a unique sacred set of music sounds that you can use to begin your clairaudience journey. The Solfeggio frequencies resonate deeply within our nature so we are prone to hold our focus a little bit longer.

Claircognizance is the subtle psychic sense of knowing things clearly. Like with every other psychic ability, the key is to bring your focus at the present moment for as much time as you can. You can enhance the empathic ability claircognizance by shifting your attention on sustaining a still mind, uninhibited of thoughts and fill it with an image of pure crystal energy. That way you will make room for the intuitive claircognizance information to flow in and your conscious mind to step aside.

Every person has innate spiritual gifts. And for most people these abilities are deeply dormant, they are deeply paralyzed because of inactivity. To make claircognizance come through, draw your focus upon clarity, quiet the rumble of the mind, capitulate your mind, dissolve your ego and you will gain the exceptional chance to touch something that exceeds the physical senses, the magnificent frequency of the spiritual world.

It's really a lot about surrendering the conscious mind and allowing the unconscious mind to come forward.

The moment you become aware that you are extracting higher information outside you, originating from the psychic realm, all your doubts whether you are capable to handle it, to understand the information will vanish. Your higher self or your spirit guides will connect to you and assist you in comprehending and the usage you can put the new information into.

Your higher self can help you to decipher what are the takeaways of the messages you are getting and how can you apply them to your current situation. And do not worry if you will lose your connection higher self. We have a post on establishing a connection with your higher self.

If you are facing difficulties with understanding the visuals or information that you are receiving, there is a high probability that it could be from the absence of an attention to the spiritual world and unused empathic abilities.

On the bright side of things, with a bit more practice of your mind and emotional faculties, you will increase your capacity to sustain your focus and maintain one state easily to channel cosmic knowledge and tune into the intuitive part of you.

Essentially your focus establishes the subtle link between you as a receiver and the psychic dimension as a sender. It is of prime importance to constantly practice and hone your skills to tune into the psychic realm as when you do not from a higher dimensional perspective your being, which is perceived as pure energy, twinkles from strong to faint and it is a challenge for your spirit guides or higher self to send you complete, greater information as in one moment you are there and the next you are gone.

Developing your empathic psychic focus to appear long enough in the higher dimensions for your spirit guides and your higher self as strong energy will not only solve your earthly problems of meeting project deadlines, being on time, getting things done but will generally make you wiser and increase your vibration to help the world be a better place.

All you need is to do it once to twice a day at a time comfortable for you.

As you advance, you will notice that you have accessed psychic information before but were unable to differentiate it from your thoughts or simply your ego took credit for it.

Your emotional body and mind will become much more stable and still of the thoughts flowing in from your spirit guides or your higher self once you start strengthening your empathic abilities.

Chapter 16: Flower Essence Remedies for Empaths

Empaths or hypersensitive persons are in tune with vibrational frequencies. They are vulnerable to taking on emotional "gunk" belonging to others which can cause them to feel anxious, fatigued, overwhelmed, or hurt. Below is a collection of flower remedies intended to help sensitive people release emotionally-charged energies and also shield themselves from picking up foreign energies in the future. Some of these essences can also help the empath work more effectively with their empathic gift.

Incorporating the use of specific flower essences can help ease feelings of overwhelm or anxiousness associated with empathic natures.

Empath Essences

✓ Olive - Revitalizer. Olive is a good remedy for anyone who is feeling the effects of fatigue or struggle. Olive can help the soothe the sensitive person who takes on more than his share of suffering.

- ✓ Yarrow - Energy Shield. Yarrow is a stabilizing remedy. It can help to shield anyone who is extra sensitive or vulnerable from energies that could deplete their personal space.

- ✓ Beech - Beech remedy can serve as an energetic buffer, protecting sensitives from emotional attacks. Helpful essence remedy for anyone who feels socially vulnerable.

- ✓ Mountain Pennyroyal - Moutain Pennyroyal remedy is a protective agent that gives clarity of mind and blocks negative energies. It can also assist the empath to cleanse and purge energies that have already been picked up. Expels negativity and psychic attachments.

- ✓ Pink Yarrow - Pink Yarrow remedy helps anyone needing to create emotional boundaries. It allows a person to remain compassionate to the needs of others without taking on their burdens.

- ✓ Dandelion - Dandelion remedy serves as a laundering service for washing away painful emotions. It allows emotional sludge to move through the body and get tossed away much like how dirt gets removed from clothing when it is laundered.

- ✓ Borage - Borage is a heart healer. Sensitive persons are often heavily burdened with the emotional hurts of many. This makes borage the "go-to" remedy to ease the strain on the heart chakra. Borage lifts any burdens, offering energetic "lightness" and "healing."

- ✓ Heather - Heather is normally prescribed for the self-absorbed personality helping him to learn how to step outside of the self and become more feeling of others. For this reason, the suggestion of heather for the empath may seem to be at odds. However, heather can also help an empath sort out his emotions from adopted emotions that are not his. It helps a person recognize emotional energies in the body that do not belong.

✓ Fawn Lily - Fawn Lily essence helps reintroduce the "reclusive" personality back into the world. This remedy is an excellent aid for the empath who has kept himself locked away from others as a protective mechanism, but who wants to begin to mingle with people on his own terms in a controlled environment.

✓ Mallow - Mallow remedy helps break down self-protective walls an empath has built around himself. The problem with a solidly built energetic shield is that it not only blocks hurtful emotions, but it will block good emotions too, such as love and compassion. Mallow can help the isolated empath release fear and open up his heart so that he can begin feeling again.

✓ Yellow Star Tulip - Yellow Star Tulip is an excellent remedy for the empath who wants to use his empathic talents in the role of a healer. This remedy will help to enhance the empaths natural ability. This can be of great assistance to the healer in helping identify the needs of his clients. Refines inner truth and knowledge.

✓ Manzanita - Manzanita is a remedy for the individual who has over-identified with his spiritual nature, choosing to ignore his human side. Empaths sometimes have difficulty embracing their physical bodies because of the emotional-body connection. The spiritual body has a natural detachment from the emotional body. However, earth incarnation requires having a body and ignoring the body is not healthy. Manzanita essence helps to integrate spiritual and physical, helping the sensitive soul to view the world in a more balanced way.

Balance is a gift that flower essences offer. They assist us in creating gentle energy shifts, easing any imbalances back into check.

Conclusion

Being an empath is a gift. Like all gifts, there are challenges that come with this responsibility. Empaths are prone to health challenges such as fatigue, dizziness, and digestive problems. Additionally, they can be prone to both depression and anxiety. Energy overloads them causing them to withdraw.

You don't need to hide from the world. You're meant to be a shining light of love.

As an empath, it is essential to limit your exposure to negative influences such as dramatic news stories and people who spout anger and hate. However, you also need to stay in contact with this world and not just bury your heads in the sand.

One way to find a balance and purpose is to realize that, while you can't solve the world's problems, you can make a difference. You can choose a path of healing for your world and ourselves. While you can't give all the money and time you would like, you can choose a cause to support with your precious time and your limited resources.

When you focus on what you can do, and remind yourself of the good you have achieved, this can lift the sadness and grief and help you to feel more positive in the face of the world's problems. Even the smallest act of love and kindness can have a ripple effect on the people around you. In fact, you never know when a simple kind word or deed might change another person's life.

More and more, life reveals what a gift empathy truly is. Because you feel what others are feeling, you communicate in a way that others can sincerely relate to. Connecting on this deeper level opens up a powerful, healing space that allows for transformation, often at an accelerated pace.

Once you learn to take care of ourselves, you have so many wonderful gifts to offer the world—especially when it comes to supporting people in healing and transformation. The biggest gift of all by far is learning to trust your intuition more than anything else: knowing in your heart of all hearts that it always knows the way.

Your notes:

Recommended Readings ...

EMOTIONAL INTELLIGENCE
UNDERSTANDING THE IMPORTANCE OF EMOTIONAL INTELLIGENCE, DEVELOPING AND USING IT TO LIVE A BETTER LIFE, AND TO ENSURE ADVANCEMENT IN YOUR CAREER
RICHARD GOODMIND GOTMAN

9 781708 668082